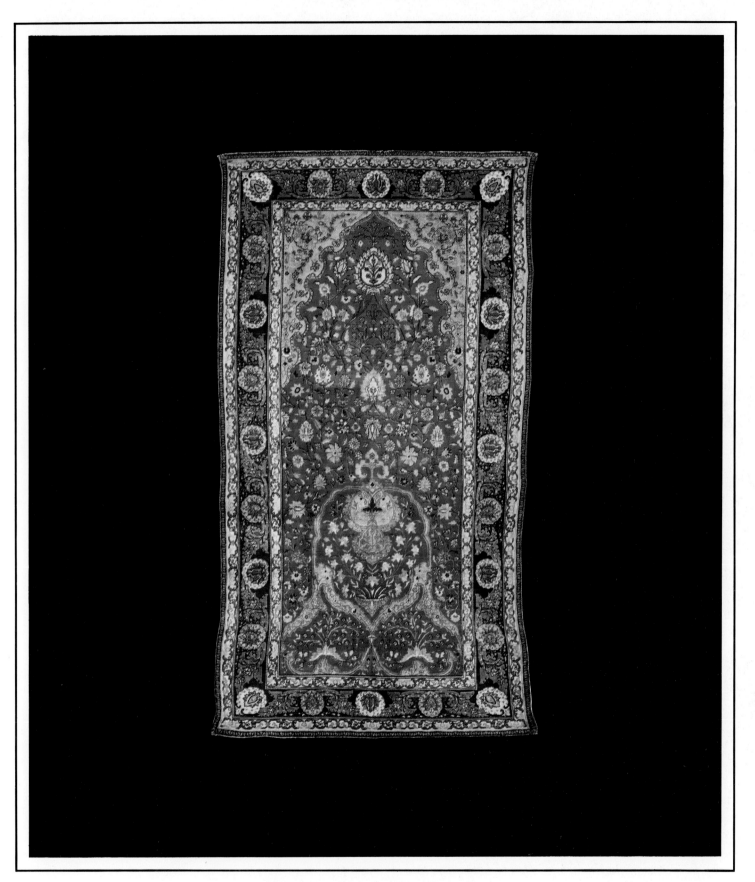

Oriental Carpets

82

Oriental Carpets

ULRICH SCHÜRMANN

This edition first published 1979 by
Octopus Books Limited,
59 Grosvenor Street,
London W1

© Ebeling Publishing Ltd., Windsor, United Kingdom
All rights reserved

ISBN 0 7064 1017 3

Colour origination by
Scala Istituto Fotografico Editoriale, Florence
Printed and bound by
Nuova Grafica Moderna, Verona, Italy

CONTENTS

Introduction

The rug as a work of art has hitherto not enjoyed the attention it deserves in modern life.

It shares this fate with all the other objects of daily life which, as the creations of artists both great and small, used to enjoy the admiration and patronage of the upper classes. One only has to think back to the high standards laid down for the craftsmen's guilds in the Ancient World and Middle Ages. The bronze vessels, glass goblets, silver beakers, porcelain bowls and the thousands of other objects in daily use were also highly treasured works of art. They were yardsticks for the wealth, background and taste of the owner. On the one hand there was the small group of nobles, or upper classes, and on the other, the mass of ordinary people, who were in no position to afford such objects and who had to make do with the simplest of materials.

Since then, things have changed radically. As a result of industrial progress and social reform, everyone nowadays in all civilized countries has the material chance and intellectual stimulus to appreciate and possibly even to acquire works of art. However, the world is being flooded with mass-produced goods which contradict the notion of everyday articles as works of art. Gold- and silversmiths, carpenters, bookbinders, glassblowers, to mention but a few of the old craftsmen, have seen their crafts decimated and are now having to fight for their survival in a world in which ostensibly similar products are machine-made at a fraction of the price.

It is only in recent years that the rug has shown signs of a rebirth. In the United States, many collectors' clubs and associations have been formed. The Washington Textile Museum is enjoying increasing importance and recognition. Exhibitions of rugs have been held in Hamburg, Frankfurt-on-Main, Munich and London as well as in many cities of the USA. The McMullan

Collection, one of the most important private collections, was shown in Frankfurt-on-Main in 1968, and then later in London.

In a discussion on the oriental rug as a work of art, some attempt should be made to define 'art' in this context. Unfortunately space does not permit a survey of the manifold theories put forward in the past to arrive at a definition. Suffice it to say, therefore, that command of technique does not alone mean art. It is much more important for the artist to infuse something of the 'divine' into the object he is creating. It is this innate, elementary force which finds its expression in the primitive oriental rug of the nomads as well as in the courtly design of luxury carpets, which is so important.

In addition, one must consider the effect that the rug has on the beholder. It is not even necessary for the individual to 'understand' the work of art. It is sufficient if his eye is pleased and his heart gladdened.

Rugs have much in common with paintings. A rug has a central field and a border, just as a painting is enclosed by its frame. Like the painter, the nomadic weaver tries to transpose nature's ever-changing play of colour from the three-dimensional to the two-dimensional. Surrounded by rugged, treeless mountains or endless, arid steppe, the artist endeavours to conjure up, either for himself or for others, a garden to help him forget the surrounding landscape. Just as a painting can be the focal point in a room and can delight a person or induce thought, so a rug should embellish the life of its owner, as well as giving the rich pleasure in possessing an object of value and taste.

The oriental rug was not used in the way Europeans would understand it to be used, but formed a central theme in everyday life. As a result, it was well cared for and looked after. In the rooms of the wealthy it was the focal point, surrounded by runners which were walked or sat upon. The rug was for looking at, for hanging in the nomads' tents, and sometimes even became the desirable dowry of an astute bride.

The rug possesses two other qualities, both of which distinguish it from a painting. When one looks at a picture from all angles and in all kinds of light, it hardly changes. A rug, however, takes its 'glow' from the pile—the direction of the wool or silk. If the pile runs with the light, the colours appear lighter and more harmonious. If one looks into the pile against the light, the colours are stronger, darker and in greater contrast to each other.

Again in contrast to the picture, the rug calls yet another of our senses into play, that is the sense of touch. The feel of a rug or, technically speaking, the 'handle' of a rug is most important. The owners of old rugs can experience the most remarkable sensations simply by touching, grasping or stroking them; real experts can even assess the age of a rug by its handle. Touching a really old Tekke (Bokhara) carpet, stroking a 100-year-old Kashan rug, and fondling the silk of a 'Polish Rug' all evoke feelings of well-being and pleasure that a picture cannot produce. It is not surprising, therefore, that the true connoisseur, when selecting rugs for purchase, does not have them laid out for him, but takes hold of each rug himself. The quality of wool or silk and the fineness of stitch will thus be assessed by his hands.

How does one become a connoisseur? As for all aspects of visual art, it is principally the eye that must be trained. The more opportunity the collector has to visit museums, auctions and dealers, so much the better. Every reasonable dealer will allow the budding collector to examine his rugs. But first, one should get hold of literature on the subject which has been amplified by many new works over the last few years, and which gives the reader a theoretical insight at least into the world of the oriental rug. Some knowledge of the different weaving and knotting techniques, and of the basic structure is also needed, as these details give reliable indications regarding the origin of the rug. In addition, a little knowledge of the history of the tribes who made the rugs will also lead to a better understanding and appreciation.

The budding collector is often tempted to classify ornamentation and to interpret symbols. It is unquestionably true to say that symbolism dominates in many pieces, especially in those from East Asia. It is equally true that the nomad or peasant woman endeavoured to weave into the rug something from her own experience of life. One should not, however, dwell too long on the details of the ornamentation and its symbolism to the detriment of the whole. Let everyone read into the rug what his fantasy tells him, as long as it remains, in its entirety, a permanent source of pleasure.

Designs—straight or curved lines

Carpets are textile products and, being such, are exposed more than any other antique art to the ravages of the laws of nature, that is, to decay. One can, therefore, never establish definitely when the first woven rug was made. It must be assumed, of course, that the weaving process had already been invented—an invention that may well have been one of the earliest of mankind. It is generally assumed that the carpet was originally intended to replace animals' pelts. It is therefore reasonable to assume that originally a thick, woollen texture was produced, whose monotony man—ever desirous of beauty—strived to alleviate by means of a design.

In the beginning, one probably just inserted long, coloured woollen threads into a backing; these were used as pattern-forming threads, as their further development shows. Their shagginess made them resemble the original animal fur more closely. As warp and weft threads meet at right angles in the weave, the first patterns may well have been dictated by this, i.e. they were criss-cross lines in alternating colours. From these primitive patterns evolved more complicated textures over periods of time—how long it took is guesswork—which allowed more scope for the imagination by using interlacing and shorn yarns or yarn threads. The shagginess of the old carpet gave way to a plush-like or velvety surface.

It was only the discovery of the knot, however, which elevated the product to a level which permitted a rapid development in patterning. There is an essential distinction in the Orient between two sorts of knot, the so-called Ghiordes or Turkish knot, and the Persian or Senneh knot. They differ in that, in the Ghiordes knot, the wool is taken over two warp threads and then stands up like a woolly bunch in the middle of these two warp threads; in the Persian knot, although the woollen thread is still passed over

11

two warp threads, only one thread stands up between these two warp threads. It was not so long ago that the Turkish knot was thought to be the older, and the Persian the younger. But the discoveries in the ice-tombs of the Altai have proved that there were knotted rugs as early as approximately 500 BC. These showed not only an astonishing degree of artistic representation, but also the existence of both types of knot. If one looks at these earliest known products of the art of knotting, one must necessarily come to the conclusion that, even before these, there must have been a centuries-old period of development. The famous Pazyryk rug shows in its design and harmony of colours, as well as in the fineness of its stitch, such a high degree of the art of knotting that it can hardly be surpassed by products from the classical period, or 'Golden Age', of Persian weaving—that is to say, of the 15th and 16th centuries. There are so few examples from the period 500 BC to AD 1400 that one cannot form a true picture of the real extent of the art of weaving rugs during these 2,000 years.

If the usual view is adopted, that the cradle of the woven rug was to be found in central Asia or the old Urartu, known today as Azerbaijan, then in all probability it was the Turkish knot that predominated in the oldest known rugs. The use of the Turkish knot would also appear to be the logical sequel to the straight lines of more primitive textures. Due to the gaps between the warps, the knot does not lend itself to curved lines, but only to straight or staggered ones. This is borne out, too, by the few examples of early woven rugs of the pre-Islamic period up to the 15th century, when they were replaced by transcriptions of book ornamentations and illustrations of a courtly style. Thus we find rugs of geometrical design in the Persian town of Herat at the time of the Timerides, and only later do we gradually come across curved ornaments. In the early miniatures of Bokhara, Herat and India, all rugs are drawn geometrically although floral touches sometimes appear within the lozenges and rectangles.

Up to the middle of the 19th century, that is before European influences 'estranged' the Oriental rug, there were clearly defined ethnological areas where straight lines were the predominant characteristic. This applies mainly to those regions where Turcomen tribes had settled. But other peoples, such as the Armenians and Egyptians, joined forces with this group. Thus all Anatolian rugs—with the exception of those produced in the court workshops of Istanbul or its vicinity, which were subject to Osman influence —were divided up strictly geometrically. The many tribes of the Caucasus exploited the variations of geometrical design to the highest perfection, whilst the Turk tribes in Persia, who were nomads in the south and the west of the country, likewise restricted themselves to geometrical ornamentation. To them belong the Afshari, the Shiras, the Kashgai, the Luris and the Kurds. During the 19th century however, floral ornaments frequently found their way into the purely geometrical style, and so one can find some woven pieces containing a *mélange* of both tendencies.

Further towards the east were those who kept to the straight line for as long as we know—the Turcomen tribes of Turkestan in particular—and who preferred their own range of reds in the colour scale. The tribes of the Tekke, Saryk, Yomud and Ersari knew how to produce works of art with a minimum use of colour, yet with a subtlety of nuance which always retained their tribal *güls* (decorative devices).

The Turkestan tribes from the Tarim Basin wove rugs which, whilst observing the laws of geometry, often reproduced plant designs. Above all it is the rugs from Khotan and Yarkand whose effect is most convincing by virtue of their magnificent colours and strict lines. Kashgar, on the other hand was, for the East

Turkestan rug, what Istanbul was for the Turkish carpet. Where-ever courtly art and a more elegant life-style were possible in cultured society, straight lines alone did not seem to suffice. The ornamentation of Osman court workshops and that of the Kashgar rugs show in the early stages of their development the first signs of a curve, which subsequently led to the perfection of floral shapes.

Scarcely anything remains from the early times of China and Mongolia. In any case, the archaic rugs of this district, known to us only from illustrations, are of strict geometric form. Their range of colours is limited to a harmony of blue, yellow and apricot. The economy of their open design, together with their pastel colourings, makes these rugs quite unmistakable.

Nothing illustrates more clearly than the products of Cairo the transition from the 'straight' to the 'curved' line. Up to the conquest by the Turks in the middle of the 16th century, a linear ornamentation dominated the rug which reached the culmination of its artistic form in the restrained use of colours (green, yellow, red and some blue). One only needs to think of the famous silk rug of the Mamelukes in Vienna, or the Simonetti rug recently acquired by the Metropolitan Museum in New York. They represent that which is most refined and striking in art to have been achieved with straight lines and a minimum of colour.

With the conquest by the Osmans this type of decoration ceased and its place was taken by the court art of Istanbul. Whilst the range of colours remained for one more century, the straight line became the curved line. Rugs with an abundance of flowers with lancet-shaped leaves and curved prayer niches characterize the new era. Istanbul with its workshops, Brousa and a few other places in Asia Minor all adopted the new trend. It is therefore all the more surprising that, at the same time, rugs woven by nomads and farmers of Anatolia have retained their geometric patterning right up to the present day.

A similar development can be seen in Spain. Up to the 15th century, the magnificent rugs brought into Spain by Arabian tribes as part of their art show a geometrical design. It was primarily in the workshops of the Alcaras that excellent specimens using straight lines were made which almost matched up in beauty and harmony of colour with Egyptian products. But here, too, the same change is apparent after the 16th century; curved lines and floral designs, but with a much smaller choice of colours, (mostly yellow with green, or yellow with blue) became predominant in the rugs and replaced the geometrical art of Arabia.

Undoubtedly the culmination of floral ornamentation and the supremacy of the curved line was attained in Central Persia towards the end of the 15th and in the 16th centuries. It was thanks to the Senneh knot, allowing for a delicately curved line, that the masterpieces of the oriental art of weaving came about which, from the earliest times, have delighted the connoisseur. Gifted artists adapted the book illustrations and the perfectly executed book covers for the ornamentation of rugs. They created the famous rugs which can be admired in museums all over the world, and which, by their ornamentation, have been grouped as tendril rugs, vase rugs, hunting carpets, animal carpets, etc. As the design became more sophisticated, so the colour range increased, giving rise to the creation of works of art which, in their beauty and harmony of colour, are by no means inferior to paintings. In Persia, the straight and the curved line can be found side by side right up to the present day, although a Persian rug, compared with a Caucasian, Anatolian and Turkoman rug, favours a more curved type of line, even in rural districts.

The conclusion to be drawn from this would appear to be that the straight line is the spiritual preserve of nomads and farmers, whereas the curved line presupposes an urbane, courtly and perhaps even a more decadent form of society. In both groups are to be found highlights of artistic expression, elevating them above the welter of everyday products.

Yet considering all this one must not forget that the oriental rug in its non-courtly form can be regarded as an expression, or even as the handwriting of the people. In earlier times, probably nearly all male and female weavers could neither read nor write. Because they were illiterate they wove into the carpet the whole range of their imagination, as well as the expression of their temperament and feelings. And so the old carpet is a reflection of its maker. Even if each rug seems to have been woven by the same tribe in the same way, there are in fact differences in shades, fineness of stitch, colour composition, arrangement of the traditional ornaments, or just in the care with which it has been woven.

Colours–bold or subtle

In painting, even the amateur art critic can recognize the origin or age of a picture by its colour composition. The subdued magnificence of the colours of the Italian School of the 16th century differs unmistakably from the Dutch paintings of the 17th century. The scintillating colours of the Impressionists are very different from the dark, glowing colours of 17th century Spanish painters. In the realm of the oriental rug, there has been less of a change of mood, as regards colour than a preservation—through the centuries—of the characteristics of the colour scale of the individual rug-producing tribe. And so one can determine the origin of a rug not only by its knot, wool or design, but also by its colour composition. Nor would it be wrong here to interpret the carpet as the reflection of a people's character, temperament and imagination together with its creative power of expression in the colours.

First of all mention must be made of the innate boldness of the Caucasian rug which appears most convincing and pleasing to the modern beholder. There are Caucasian rugs in which the juxtaposition of colour contrasts is extremely daringly made, and yet the overall impression is one of a harmonious burst of colour.

It is not the contrast in colours—however striking it may be—which offends the eye, but the misuse of colours. The colours of an east Turkestan rug using aniline dyes are considered displeasing because they have lost their original colour values. The charm of a Khotan or Kashgar from before 1860 degenerates 50 years later into a frightening caricature. All oriental rugs woven before 1860 possess a harmony of colour regardless of whether they are 'gentle' or 'bold'. Later products frequently represent only garish, sometimes startling imitations of a bygone epoch of folk art. People have, therefore, sometimes attempted to achieve the former charm and patina of great age by chemical washing.

Though by doing this the dull ugliness of the crass colours has been softened, one has simply replaced one evil by another. Throughout the history of art there have always been periods when artists or peoples produced masterpieces which could neither be replaced nor repeated. One may well copy them, but mere copies cannot offer the beholder the same pleasure as the original.

In this context it should be pointed out that the collector ought never to be tempted by the expert and stylistically accurate forgery. Apart from other indications it is the colour in particular which gives away a forgery. The translucency of colours in a genuine antique carpet is so great that the carpet appears almost to be rising from the floor, and the beholder is spellbound by its irresistible charm. The colours of the forged rug are dull, the wool lifeless, and a sort of veil seems to cover the piece. If the beholder has to stop and think whether or not the piece is genuine or forged, then it is forged. The genuine rug seems to speak to the beholder, and does not even permit doubts of logical reflection.

Whilst the Caucasian rug with its expressionist colouring takes first place for wild abandon of colour, it is the Anatolian rug which follows. It is above all the contrasts of red and blue with the addition of a clear, shining yellow, that determine the colour scale. It is therefore not surprising that the collector of Caucasian rugs is often also a collector of Anatolian ones.

Next comes the Persian rug, with its wealth of colours and shades. Its colours do not stand in contrast to one another, but are carefully gradated. Thus a sophistication of harmony is achieved which is not only pleasing to the eye, but also offers the greatest flexibility for use in modern interiors. Here the beholder is delighted not by the primitive wildness of colour, but by the all-embracing elegance of the spectrum.

In contrast to these groups, the 'subtle' colours should be mentioned—'subtle' inasmuch as an artistic effect has been obtained by using as few colours as possible. Here we have above all the Turkoman rugs comprising the region of Turkestan and Afghanistan, as well as parts of northern Persia, whose colour range is dominated by an infinite variation of reds which are set against a gentle, non-contrasting, dark blue. In addition one finds here and there browns from undyed camel hair, which round off the range. One never ceases to be amazed with what scarcity of means a colourful, pleasing and artistically satisfying picture could be produced.

Further to the east, in east Turkestan and China, it is the pastel shades which afford a charming ensemble by their muted harmony. Whereas red is still largely used as the basic colour in east Turkestan rugs, Chinese rugs are restricted to shades which exclude a true red. The imperial yellow together with apricot and pale blue dominate the rug. In addition there are a few ornaments in various shades of grey. The colour effect of these rugs seems to mirror the philosophical tranquillity and equanimity of this ancient civilization.

Oddly enough it is Spain of the 16th and 17th centuries which, similarly to east Turkestan and China, keeps its use of colour to a minimum. Almost all rugs of this epoch have green or pastel blue floral ornaments on a pale yellow ground.

Between Persia and its wealth of colours, and east Turkestan with its subtle composition, lies India. It was the Mogul rulers who, at the beginning of the 16th century, introduced the Persian art of weaving into this country. In the course of one century India developed a distinctive colour range, the most outstanding characteristic of which is a strong, glowing cherry red. Against this basic shade is contrasted a trellis pattern filled with flowers, depicting in shades of green, yellow and blue realistic flowering shrubs. In their effect the carpets make one think of the burning sun of India.

A trait common to all oriental rugs, be they bold or subtle, is the inexplicably mysterious charm they exert over us. The veil of this mystery may perhaps be lifted somewhat, if one realizes that every colour in the rug which at first glance appears as a single colour, is actually composed of many colour shades of the same basic colour. Every square centimetre contains a number of variations of the same shade, due to differences in the quality of the wool and its thickness, as well as to differences in the dyeing methods. Even the most experienced dyer cannot dye two hanks of wool to exactly the same colour. It is just these delicate shadings that give life and a unique charm to the carpet. If this same carpet were dyed with absolutely constant colours, and if the wool used were mechanically spun and twisted into a flawless yarn, the effect would be boring. It would be similar to the machine-made carpets which came on to the market in the 1920s as copies of oriental rugs.

In less carefully worked pieces one frequently encounters colour gradations which are so strong as to represent an obvious break with the colour scale. This is called 'abrash'. As long as it is kept within reasonable limits, the 'abrash' adds interest to the carpet, and should not be looked upon as a fault. It is only when such colour gradations form a complete change of colour and not merely a change of shade, that the carpet suffers.

There is no accounting for taste. Whilst there is a preference in Germany for the 'bold', that is, carpets from the Caucasus and Anatolia (perhaps also with additional pieces from Turkestan), other countries prefer the 'subtle'. These combine Chinese with east Turkestan and Spanish carpets. However, all countries have a love of the Persian carpet. According to our idea of taste, the 'bold' and the 'subtle' are usually incompatible in one room. The expression and creative power of peoples are as different as the peoples themselves, and so one has to treat each group of carpets individually, just as the group of people which produced them.

Animal and floral motifs

In pre-Islamic times there were no restrictions placed on the ornamentation of carpets. As we can see from the example of the early Pazyryk carpet, floral and animal depictions were combined. Because the carpet included in its design things from everyday life and nature, it is not surprising that, in addition to plant life, animals were also depicted, as well as household objects and tools which served in the production of the carpets (shears, combs, etc.). Down the centuries these depictions have become so abstract as to be almost unrecognizable, and only in very rare instances, by looking at particularly old pieces, is it possible to trace the development of an ornament. Scientists who have made studies in the weaving areas in the last 30 years report that to a large extent the weavers themselves no longer know what a particular ornament is supposed to represent or what it has developed from.

Just as one can tell the different weaving areas by their geometric or floral patterning, by bold or subdued colours, so too does the predominance of floral or animal ornaments reveal the country of origin and the age of the carpet.

Starting with Anatolia, the paintings of the Gothic age show that carpets were made there in which dragons, birds and fabulous creatures were depicted. One cannot help thinking that they are the same animals encountered in early Chinese carpets—dragon, phoenix, lion, temple guard dog, etc. Obviously there was an exchange of ideas and ornamentation within Asia, which stimulated the thoughts of the weavers along the 'Silk Route' from east to west and west to east. In later centuries one no longer finds animals in Anatolian carpets. Floral ornaments predominate in peasant products as well as in goods ordered by and made for the court.

In the Caucasus, too, there was a definite period in which the pattern of the dragon, phoenix and of other animals was very popular, although this period does not run parallel to that of Anatolia. These are the well loved and much sought-after 'dragon' carpets of the 17th century. They are followed in the 18th and 19th centuries by the most beautiful and valuable examples of the Caucasian art of weaving, where, strewn amongst purely geometrical ornaments, birds, domestic animals and sometimes human figures can be found. The floral ornament in these carpets is abstracted and geometrized to such an extent that, apart from flowering shrubs, hardly a floral motif remains clearly recognizable as such.

In Central Asian Turkestan, so few really antique carpets are preserved that it appears almost impossible to interpret individual ornaments as being either of floral or animal nature. The Russian scholar Gogel assumes, for example, that the divisions of a Tekke *gül* represent a fenced-in grazing ground interspersed with canals and trees. In some very old Yomud rugs the supposed leaf designs can be traced back to abstracted butterflies and bats. In the so-called 'Tauk Nuska' *güls*, four-legged, horned animals are depicted, the origin of which is disputable. Yet the floral pattern of the three-leaf motif remains predominant. In the border, too, the ever prevalent, typically oriental blossom-and-leaf tendril design occurs, but frequently so distorted that practically only a meandering line is left. It is only at the ends of early Tekke and Yomud carpets that clearly defined floral ornamentation is found. The older the carpet, the more realistic are the flowering shrubs or fir-tree-like ornamentations which embellish the 'apron' of the rug. The Turkoman tribes of Turkestan produced carpets with geometric floral patterns and carpets in which additional animal patterns have become distorted beyond recognition.

Their neighbours in east Turkestan were pure vegetarians. There is such an abundance of blossoms, flowering shrubs, pomegranate trees and rosettes that there is no room left for animal reproductions. The vase is encountered time and time again in many carpets as an object of handicraft.

In the Chinese carpet the naturalistic reproduction of floral ornaments (lotus blossoms, peonies, chrysanthemums) has been carried to stylistic perfection. Although the floral design predominates, there are also certain animal depictions which appear in carpets designed mostly for a specific use. Thus the dragon occurs very frequently in column carpets, and a circle of lions and temple dogs appears in the middle of predominantly floral carpets and blends unobtrusively into the floral picture.

There is a small group of some very early Chinese carpets, in which the motif of the dragon, thinly and geometrically drawn, is intentionally emphasized, either as a continuous pattern, or as an opposed pattern. It is only in the 19th century that realistic depictions of symbolic meaning creep into the patterning where horses in various positions and deer are to be seen. But the original, characteristic Chinese carpet is the floral carpet.

Persia is a special case in that the depiction of humans and animals was undesirable for religious reasons. Thus the Persian carpet, with the exception of the famous animal and hunting carpets of the 16th century, restricts itself to floral patterns which are astonishing in their abundance of variations. Erdmann and Wiener Werk show tendril sketches which evoke the greatest respect for the task the weaver was faced with. Frequently two or three trellis systems are superimposed and only careful analysis makes it possible to discern the complicated tracery which is swallowed up by the wealth of ornament and colour when looking at the carpet as a whole. One can be fairly certain in assuming that carpets with animal depictions or even hunting scenes were woven in the court workshops only to order for the most important personages. In the vast weaving areas of Persia, however, the floral pattern was the only one which, in inexhaustible variations, formed the decoration of the Persian rug.

One would appear to be justified in concluding that generally in the oriental carpet the floral motif was not only predominant, but also the most suitable from the technical aspect, and that rugs with essentially animal depictions were produced over relatively short periods. Ultimately the carpet signifies for the Oriental, living in a mostly arid, stony and steppe-like environment, the fulfillment of a wish to call his own a three-dimensional garden in two-dimensional form. The pride and wealth of the garden owner expresses itself in the beauty, magnificence of colour and quality of the carpet which, as the centrepiece of the room, is gazed upon with admiration and lovingly cared for.

Symbolism

How often is the question of what a particular decoration means asked when ornaments appear in a carpet, the significance and origin of which leave the collector's thirst for knowledge unassuaged. Answering such questions can lead to extraordinary difficulties and any interpretation of the ornaments can only be, at best, a non-committal guess.

In Chinese rugs above all, symbolism has been taken to its utmost perfection. A people that can give a symbolic meaning to every colour and to every object has also used ornaments and colours in its rugs and given them a symbolic significance in addition to their factual representation. The naturalistic reproduction of such objects easily permits this explanation. All that is necessary is a thorough knowledge of the Chinese way of life and attitude to life. Many of these symbols have found their way to the West and have been rediscovered in variations, frequently so abstracted as to be unrecognizable, in carpets from Persia, the Caucasus and Anatolia. To these belong, amongst others, the cloud band, the chintamani and the dragon-phoenix motif. Whether the meander border in its many different forms came from Greece to Asia or *vice versa*, is open to conjecture. The 'running dog' border, particularly well known from Caucasian carpets of the 19th century, can also be found in very old fragments from Egypt and Central Asia. It could have stemmed from the wave crests of old Chinese and east Turkestan rugs.

To what extremes an attempt at interpretation can go may be illustrated by a little anecdote. In the famous Türk ve Islam Eserleri Müzesi in Istanbul, an artist has been busy for many years copying onto graph paper, knot for knot, the carpets from the museum's stocks. Thus he must have had a profound knowledge of all their details. During a conversation the question came up about the meaning of the well known leaf-calyx border, as is frequently found in Caucasian and Anatolian rugs. Surprisingly, the artist was of the opinion that the leaves on the right and left of the calyx represented a dog viewed from the side, and the calyx itself a dog seen from the front. There were no further questions asked.

The Armenians pride themselves in believing that the discovery of the art of weaving rugs and its spread over the whole of the Near East is entirely attributable to them. Books have been written in which all ornaments have been traced back to Armenian objects, customs and religious beliefs. Any cross-like shape in a carpet is sufficient for an Armenian to state that the piece was conceived and woven by Armenians.

In contrast, the author has so far declined in all his publications to express any opinion on this point of symbolism. He believes it should be left to the beholder alone to read into the carpet what he wants to see in it. Let us consider it as an entity, take pleasure in the abundance of colour and ornament, in the mysterious signs of bygone ages, and live with the carpet as a magical mystery which can surprise us from one day to the next by new and unsuspected aspects of its beauty.

Depth of pile and density of knotting

The budding collector is often tempted to attach unjustifiably great importance to fineness of stitch of a carpet and the attendant height of pile. In reality, the structure of a carpet depends to a large extent on where it was woven and for what purpose. One might almost say it is climatically conditioned. What this really means can be explained most clearly if one takes the Caucasian carpet as an example. These rugs, woven in the valleys of the Caucasus under severe climatic conditions, are primarily intended to yield warmth. Thus they are coarse in weave and have a high pile. To these belong the Kazak, Karabagh and Gendje. In the plain which extends from the east of the Caucasus along the Caspian Sea, which has a milder climate, thinner, finer carpets are woven with a much more clearly defined pattern because of the shorter pile. The deciding factor is, of course, centuries-old tradition as well as tribal and racial peculiarities. Thus it is the carpets woven by the Tartars (Moghan, Saliani, Talish), incredibly fine of stitch, and using brilliant colours with a low-cut pile, that belong to the most attractive of Caucasian rugs.

In the same way the finest Turkish carpets made by the court workshops around Istanbul, with their extremely low-cut pile, contrast with the rugs woven by the nomads and farmers of Anatolia, of which typical examples are the well known and popular Bergamos with their high pile and coarse weave. Carpets of medium pile height are concentrated in and around central Anatolia (Kula, Ghiordes, Mujur, Ladik, etc.). The nearer one gets to the mountainous region of the Caucasus, the higher the pile becomes and the coarser and firmer the weave. This is particularly true of the Kars rug, outwardly very similar in design and colouring to products of the adjoining Kazak district.

It is because of the climatic conditions in one mountainous region of Persia that one finds the high-pile Kurdish carpets. They differ from the finely woven, short-shorn rugs of central Persia (Feraghan, Senneh, Isfahan, Tehran, etc.), as well as from the carpets ordered by and for the court, designed by artists as luxury articles for a small upper class.

Similar conditions apply to Turkestan and Afghanistan. The Tekke and Salor rugs woven in the wide steppes of Turkestan have a lower pile and are more finely knotted than the rugs from the mountainous north of Afghanistan. Yomud rugs have a higher pile—a tribal peculiarity—than the Ersari of Turkestan, which favour a relatively low pile and a more open texture.

The Kashgar rugs of east Turkestan have the lowest pile, as a result of the influences of court and town. Then come the Yarkand rugs with their firm backing and low pile and in contrast to them the Khotan rugs featuring looser weave and higher pile.

The Agra carpets from India have a very strong backing and relatively high pile, whilst the products from Lahore and other weaving centres of Northern India have tweedy backings and extremely low-cut piles.

To a certain extent Chinese carpets have a special place. The older the carpet is, the coarser and looser the backing with a relatively high, shaggy pile. The best examples are the early Ning Hsia. Mongolian rugs are firmer and thicker in their backing. The later rugs from Pao-Tao and Peking have a finer backing and high pile; but these cannot really be regarded as products of folk art, for they were produced in workshops, and their pile could be shorn to any specified height.

For the experienced collector, neither the fineness of a rug nor the height of the pile is the decisive factor. A coarse, shaggy, Sino-Tibetan rug of the 17th century can, as far as the collector is concerned, be much more valuable than a finely woven Senneh rug of the 19th century. As a work of art, a coarsely woven, high pile Bergamo can far surpass in its abstract composition and richness of colour the finest silk rug from the court workshops of Istanbul. A rough high-pile Kazak in massive, bold design can put the finest of Moghans with its delicately gradated colours in the shade. For the collector the only important thing should be that the piece is as perfect an example as possible of artistic creativeness with regard to design, composition and colours, and that the whole forms a harmonious picture, being moreover a representative example of the tribe or race who wove it.

We have been talking here of 'thick' and 'thin' carpets. This certainly does not mean worn carpets. A rug with a high pile that has become thin through use, has a lesser value than the collector usually realizes. A porcelain cup of the 18th century may be worth a large sum, but if this same cup has an invisible, hairline crack, ascertainable only by the sound the cup gives when lightly tapped, then the value of the cup may be only one tenth of that of a perfect example, or even less. A similar drop in value applies to carpets which are worn. Such a carpet loses not only 10 or 20 per cent of its value, but can become almost valueless. The collector should therefore rather wait, or save more money, until he can find and acquire as perfect a specimen as possible.

Obviously certain allowances must be made for classical carpets which have suffered with the passage of time. Their value is mainly governed by rarity, age, and historical interest. It appears completely understandable that a collector should want to acquire examples of groups of carpets irrespective of their condition and trade value, for reasons of purely ethnological and historical interest.

Ways of determining the age

Experience alone, gained over the years, engenders the right feeling for the age of a carpet. As for all works of art and handicraft, the expert's knowledge is based on sight and comparison. The initial incomprehensible confusion of quality, styles and periods suddenly clears up overnight. Love of the subject and a natural flair, as in all studies, play a considerable part here.

In contrast to other aspects of art the carpet reveals more criteria on which to base one's judgment; for with no other object of artistic creation do touch, handle and feel play such important parts in assessing age.

Quite apart from deliberate forgeries, it is first of all the stylistic overall impression that gives clues to the age of the piece. In Caucasian and Turkoman rugs, where geometrization and abstraction have proceeded apace, down the centuries, it is the older carpet in which the ornamentation is reproduced more realistically and is perhaps still recognizable. For all carpets of the Orient it is true to say that stylistic purity, careful execution of the corners and the relationship of the border to the central field are important elements in assessing age. It should be noted that really early rugs show a narrower border than later examples.

In addition to stylistic fidelity, colours can also betray the age of a carpet. The intensive clarity of an antique rug, irrespective of which area of Asia it was woven in, is a convincing guide. Even the apparently monotonous Turkoman carpets are a good example of this. The older the rug the more colourful it is. Yomud and Tekke rugs can attain such a range and intensity of colour as one would not think possible, considering the limited choice of colours in later products from this area.

An infallible characteristic in determining the age of a carpet is the colour of the yellow. The older the carpet, the clearer and purer is the yellow. In later carpets the yellow tends either to orange or to brownish hues. Other colours, too, should stand out clearly and brightly. The more the overall picture of the carpet is blurred, the more the colours appear to run into one another, the younger the carpet is. The basic condition for the intensity and clarity of the colours is the quality of the wool used. The velvety, natural sheen of old and antique rugs has survived for centuries and remains unmistakably preserved, even down to the knots in well worn pieces. This sheen represents, therefore, one of the most important indications for deciding the age.

A further help is seen in the structure of the backing. The older the texture, the more susceptible it is to climatic influences. Thus one frequently finds that really antique rugs have become brittle, or at least partially so. Sometimes it is the warp, sometimes the weft, depending on the susceptibility of the material. Certainly it is more desirable to possess an antique rug which is completely 'healthy', yet a slight sensitivity of the rug need not necessarily mean a drop in value. Naturally enough, carpets with a stiff or very closely woven backing tend to be more brittle, as folding puts a greater strain on them than on loosely knotted rugs with a soft texture. One sees all too often the bad habit some dealers and collectors have of subjecting an old carpet to a breaking test, by bending the back with both hands. The irreparable damage which such a test often causes bears no relation to the knowledge gained. If a centuries-old rug looks perfect on the back and front, that should suffice. If care is taken it will last another 100 years. If enough force is used, any carpet can be ripped apart.

A pleasing and easily ascertainable indication of the age is afforded by the make-up of the back of the carpet. Each woven texture reveals on the back fine traces of the woollen threads of the knot, which form a sort of down. This down disappears with the years through wear and the constant friction caused by the carpet simply being on the floor. If, therefore, the reverse side of the carpet is smooth and shiny, considerable age can be deduced from this. A somewhat more difficult test is to take part of the weft thread from the centre of the rug, in order to find out whether the twist and the wavy position of the warp thread remain unchanged. Recently institutions have been set up in England and Germany which are concerned with establishing scientifically the age of objects by physical and chemical means, but even if the carpet could be analysed in such a way, the result would bear no relation to the expenditure involved.

There are certain dyestuffs which by their chemical composition destroy and rot the wool of old carpets. This is particularly true of black, dark brown and green, and in Chinese rugs grey and pale orange. The length of time the process of mouldering lasts until the carpet takes on a sculptured aspect, depends not only on the age of the carpet, but also on the composition of the colours used. The stronger the corrosive material (iron or copper oxide) contained in the colour, the more quickly the woollen tufts disappear from the carpet's surface. The decomposition can go so far that even the knots disappear from the back of the carpet, leaving only the warp and the weft. It is a definite indication of the age of a carpet, but by no means accurate. After 60 or 80 years a carpet can start to show signs of mouldering, yet others take 100 years or more before this process becomes evident. Since there are also naturally coloured black and brown wools—i.e. undyed wool, from black or brown sheep, goats or camels—it is not surprising to find from time to time these colours still unaffected in really old rugs.

The forgers of antique carpets knew all about these processes. Not only did they shave the brown and black places from the copied carpet, but they also singed the back of the carpets in such a way that they appeared smooth and hairless. Nevertheless, the trained eye can spot a faked rug, even if the style has been faithfully copied. It is the colours which give the forgery away; they do not have the translucency of colour, nor does the wool possess the natural sheen. The backing is usually too stiff, and signs of wear in irregularly worn places give way to an extremely low pile extending uniformly over the surface of the carpet. The experienced collector trusts the principle that even to consider whether a rug is genuine or not suffices to regard it as a forgery. The first glance at the genuine antique carpet leaves no room for doubt at all in one's mind.

Clearly the most desirable and simplest thing would be to be able to read the age of a piece from the date woven into it. Unfortunately such indications occur only rarely. A few splendid carpets of the 'Golden Age' of Persian weaving, such as, for example, the famous Ardebil carpet in the Victoria and Albert Museum in London, are dated and occasionally one finds dates woven into Kurdish rugs of the period between the 17th and 19th centuries. The Anatolian and Caucasian rugs of the 18th and 19th centuries reveal from time to time the year in which they were produced, but in Central and East Asian pieces these are totally absent. From such dated pieces one can to a certain extent judge the age of other pieces which have no dates woven into them, provided everything else is the same in both cases. In any event, caution is called for. In the Caucasus, earlier pieces were frequently copied—for simplicity's sake from the back, as one could count the knots more easily there—in such a way that the date appears reversed on the front of the copy. In addition, the first figure, (a 1) is usually omitted, which can easily lead to the wrong conclusions.

From old pictures and miniatures one can recognize carpets which offer a certain guide to estimating the age of undated pieces.

Consequently carpets of certain periods were called after the names of the artists who painted them, (for example 'Holbein' carpets and 'Lotto' carpets). Many artists, however, used their artistic licence to depict carpets only vaguely, and to simplify complicated patterns. After all, they served merely a decorative purpose, and are not to be regarded as realistic copies of the originals. Unfortunately intensive scientific work is still lacking with regard to the depiction of carpets in paintings, for such research would produce valuable information on the development and dating of oriental carpets.

The significance of names

From time immemorial the names given to oriental rugs were as mysterious to the layman as the magic of the oriental carpet appears inexplicable. The wealth of oriental names which assail the purchaser of today is overpowering and often misleading.

Even at the beginning of scientific research into the oriental carpet, names were invented which had little or no bearing on the carpet itself or on its place of origin. Misnomers of old have stubbornly asserted themselves up to the present day. The result is that they have now come to represent certain groups of carpets which tell the expert at once what is meant, even if so far no final definition has been found as to exactly where, when and by whom the pieces were woven.

It all started in earnest with the exhibition of oriental rugs in Paris in 1878. Then one could admire a magnificent Persian carpet into which a Polish coat-of-arms had been woven. For some years it was regarded as having been produced in Poland. Ever since then these carpets have been stuck with the name 'Polish Carpet' or 'Polonaise', although it was soon realized that they had been produced in central Persia, probably in Kashan or Isfahan in the time of Shah Abbas, i.e. between about 1580 and 1620. They do not, however, seem to have been intended for Persian household use. Their frequent appearance in the inventories of the Polish and other royal households would point to the fact that they were presents from the Persian Court to foreign potentates. This is further borne out by the design and colouring which are thoroughly non-Persian. One cannot help feeling that these carpets were designed in court workshops for Europe in a style which the Persian weaver fondly imagined to be European baroque. These splendid examples were not intended for the floor but as table coverings, and for this reason a small percentage of these works of art was delivered in flat weave (*kelim* or Aubusson technique).

A surprisingly large number of these 'Polish carpets' or rather 'gift' carpets have survived the centuries—a sure sign of the high esteem in which they were held, and of how well they were stored.

A further misnomer which was widely used for many years, was that of the 'Holbein' carpets. This name had been given to early geometric Anatolian rugs of the 15th and 16th centuries, because Holbein painted them with extraordinary accuracy in his paintings. It was sheer bad luck that other carpets were also given this name which, although from the same epoch, had never been painted by Holbein. They were mostly carpets with a red ground covered by a yellow trellis pattern, and were probably woven in the same districts in the Ushak area as the 'Holbein' carpets. It is only in the last few years that these carpets have begun to be called 'Lotto' carpets, since they appear amongst others in the paintings of the artist Lorenzo Lotto.

Equally ineradicable is the designation 'Siebenbürgen' or 'Transylvanian' carpets, which is widespread for a considerable group of various qualities from Anatolia. The churches of Siebenbürgen, where the most beautiful examples of Anatolian rugs hang on the walls, are the source of this generic name. There must have been lively trade early in the 16th century between Anatolia and Siebenbürgen, of which Erdmann provides further information in his book *700 Years of Oriental Carpets*. Research into the origins of oriental carpets has since proved that these rugs came from Ushak, Ladik, Konya, Bergamo, Melas and even possibly from Smyrna. Dr May H. Beattie from Sheffield has engaged in a thorough scientific study of the 'Siebenbürgen' carpets. Her book is awaited with the greatest interest.

The examples above have been mentioned in order to show that names were made up to evade the problem of exact definition and location of the place of production.

Other designations of carpets refer to the market place where they were bought and sold, because their origin could not be ascertained. Thus for simplicity's sake, they were given the name of the place where they could be bought and from where they could be shipped. In particular, Bokhara and Samarkand belong to this group. Today we know that hardly any carpets were made in either town for export or home use. But the trade in products of many Turkoman, Yomud and Ersari tribes was concentrated in Bokhara, and these products reached Europe under the trade name of 'Bokhara'. The same applies to Samarkand, a city in which the products of Khotan, Yarkand and Kashgar were collected for sale and despatch. It is only very recently that considerable efforts have been made to throw some light on the true origin of these products.

The names which can be seen in the windows of the carpet stores could be grouped together as follows:

1 Names which reveal the place of production, i.e. Tabriz, Meriz, Meshed, Isfahan, Kerman, Feraghan, Hamadan, etc.

2 Names which reveal the size of a carpet, i.e. Zaronim, Sejadeh, Dozar, Kellehi, Exotic.

3 Names which are known for the pattern, use or shape, i.e., Namazlik, Hatchlou, Ozmolduk, Choval, Saph, star Ushak, eagle Kazak, cloudband Kazak, bird's head carpet, Riz Ghiordes (maiden carpet), cemetery rug, vase carpet, etc.

4 Names which relate to the quality, i.e. Moud, Turkbaff, Cain, Silleh Sultan, Laver, Mecca Shiraz, etc.

5 Names which are purely an arbitrary dealers' designation, i.e. Princess Bokhara, Royal Tabriz, Royal Gul Bokhara, Kiva Afghan, and others.

To exhaust the list of names and designations would fill many pages. They should be of secondary importance for the budding collector, for what's in a name? It is much more a question of the piece itself satisfying the demands of quality, harmony of colour, and composition which one comes to expect of a work of art, be it only folk art. Behind each given name hides a great range of qualities. A name cannot describe a carpet. Even a coloured photograph, let alone a black and white one, cannot convey a true impression of the real quality, the condition and the radiance of colours. Neither the layman nor the experienced collector should, therefore, acquire a carpet which he has not examined with his own eyes. Frequently he will be able to ascertain that the earlier designation given to the piece is incorrect. The name is an inadequate tag thought up by man: the overpowering beauty of the object must be allowed to speak for itself.

Building up a collection

Collecting carpets is an incurable disease. Whoever has taken more than a passing interest in oriental rugs, be it only through books, can never again free himself from their magic. He will always search for interesting and unusual pieces, and all his life he will hope for the unique 'find'.

The collector's career mostly starts with a short period of struggle. At first, his knowledge is insufficient, his eye too un-trained to be able to separate the chaff from the wheat. He should, however, not be disheartened by this, for an eventual expert may also have been tempted at the beginning into purchases he later regretted. One should nonetheless aim at replacing ruthlessly all pieces which one has obtained in ignorance, and which do not match up to the standard of the subsequent collection. It is not the quantity that makes a collection, but the quality. This applies even to the collector who places less store by the condition of the pieces, than their ethnological and historical importance. Yet examples should be avoided which are badly preserved, the wear of which detracts from the overall picture, or where considerable repair has spoilt the unity of colour. It is better to have a well preserved fragment as proof of times gone by, than an ugly worn out piece of fabric. It is moreover a strange fact that it is precisely the well preserved fragment that can lend wings to one's imagina-tion and make the piece more desirable than a complete carpet. It is often the small ornaments in a fragment which gain in significance and gladden the eye with new aspects of beauty.

When one compares several pieces, when one has the chance to select from a great number of antique carpets at a reputable dealer's (an opportunity which is becoming rarer and rarer, as the goods become scarcer), one should always decide on the carpet which makes one's heart beat faster, irrespective of value. It is, so to speak, 'love at first sight' which should make one choose with certainty the carpet which will give the owner pleasure throughout his life. It is better to save up for such a piece if the price is beyond the means of the collector, than to choose an alternative piece, simply because it is cheaper. The phrase which starts with the words 'If only I had . . .' is regrettably heard all too often.

The production areas for old and antique rugs are so widespread that the collector should choose only a small sector, in order to be able to possess nothing but the best from this specialized area. It is immaterial whether the products are of court manufacture or are true peasant or nomad rugs. The charm lies in the ability to spread out the endless variations and imaginative pleasures of a certain sector in all its fullness and beauty.

Tales from the orient

The title does not refer to the fairy stories of beautiful carpets from the 'Golden Age' of the Persian art of weaving, but to the attempts of the salesman to talk one into taking a carpet for which there is no love at first sight. Above all, be warned against the 'itinerant' dealers who pester you on the telephone for an appointment. Nowadays, this group also includes the Persian students who endeavour to fool you into believing that, thanks to their direct contacts with Persia, they can let you have rarities at very low prices. Pay no heed even if the salesman tries to tell you that the carpet he is offering is a museum piece. Under no circumstances should you be tempted by a price reduction which bears no relation to the conduct of a serious businessman. The really good old or antique rug which is worth collecting needs no convincing chatter from a salesman. It speaks its own language. Try and leave yourself enough time to visit as many cities as possible where carpets can be seen in museums. Seek out reputable carpet stores, not necessarily to buy, but to study their special pieces and to train your eye. Most dealers are pleased to see that you are interested, and will bring out their treasures from their safes. The more you can see, the more your hand can get the feel of the origin and age of a piece, the less you will have to rely on the advice of others. That does not mean that it is not worth while seeking and following the advice of specialists. They exist in every country and, once you have found them, they will be a constant source of new knowledge and happy experiences.

Capital investment and the future

Often the collector is of two minds. Not only would he like to be able to call typical examples of old or antique rugs his own, but he also wishes to be sure that the value of these carpets will increase with the passage of time—that they are in fact an 'investment'. If a banker is asked, he will reply that capital investment presupposes a returning profit, even if the value of the investment itself fluctuates. Were one to ask a car dealer, he would probably state without hesitation that a car is also a capital investment.

Antiques represent a special sphere of investment. We know that certain categories of paintings, porcelain, silver and furniture have seen an increase in value in the last 20 years which has surpassed all predictions. When one reads that a painting bought in 1950 for £1,000 reached £50,000 in an auction today, one must not think that this one instance is true for all types of *objets d'art*. For in the press reports on auctions, which one reads in the daily papers, no mention is made of the many hundreds of antique objects which are sold for the same prices, or even less than, 20 years ago. Strangely enough, it is not 'antiqueness' alone which plays a part, but fashion, too. If one happens to be in possession of a collectors' piece, which is in demand just then, one may be lucky enough to enjoy a considerable increase in value. But it is just as difficult to forecast fashion as it is to forecast an increase in value of an antique object. Of course, there are always people who have an inborn feeling for these things. But very few belong to this blessed crowd.

One thing is certain—namely, that in relation to comparable antiques of the 16th to the 19th centuries, first-class carpets in good condition have been subjected to such slight price increases, that even today such carpets can be considered as grossly undervalued. In addition, the carpet, being a textile product, is exposed to greater risks of destruction than pictures, silver or porcelain.

Natural wear, thoughtless treatment, moth damage and damp continually decimate the examples of old and antique carpets which have been handed down to us. Whatever remains that is good increases in value by that fact alone all the time. In addition, consider that the secrets of dyeing and artistic creativity are lost for ever. No new carpet, no matter how finely woven, (and which, from the point of view of handicraft, can be very expensive), can replace the mellowness of the glowing colours, or even the magic of the patina and the richness of the imagination of the weaver of an old carpet.

A new generation of collectors is growing who have not had the good fortune to become familiar with large quantities of antique rugs. Once they have succumbed to the incurable disease, there will be even fewer examples on the market. Following the law of supply and demand, old and antique carpets should really be a good capital investment, but only for as long as the piece is properly treated. If it is kept carefully rolled up in cupboards or chests to be brought out and admired from time to time, or if it is in a place, perhaps hanging on a wall, where no wear is incurred, its value is not only retained but will increase from year to year to counteract inflationary tendencies.

However, the author's view is that the real capital investment is nothing other than an investment in pleasure. Scarcely any other antique object gives the beholder, at a price he can afford, the same measure of blissful contemplation as does the oriental rug. The old or antique carpet on the floor gives daily renewed pleasure in the composition of its colours and reveals again and again new details which had escaped notice. Furthermore, it offers tranquillity and comfort and unites the other objects in the room into a decorative whole. It blends in equally well with antique and with modern interiors. One might even say that it creates excitement in the decor of a modern room, thus preventing it from being boring or impersonal. As always in life, the phrase that only the best yields the highest profit applies here, not only in actual increase in value, but also in pleasure gained from the carpet.

THE PLATES

Anatolia

The carpets knotted in the Ushak region have always been in great demand. Pictorial evidence of every style and pattern can be found from as far back as the 15th and 16th centuries in the paintings of famous artists of that time. In order to distinguish between the many different designs of rugs and identify each for the connoisseur, names have been chosen to describe them which refer either to the design itself or to the artist who reproduced it in his painting. Thus it is usual to refer to 'medallion Ushaks', 'star Ushaks', 'Holbein carpets', 'Lotto carpets', 'bird's head rugs' and 'prayer rugs'.

The example on the right is a typical 'star Ushak'. The precise, regular design and the narrow border are indications of its age. This finely knotted carpet, with its gleaming colours, can confidently be placed in the 16th century.

Anatolia. Star Ushak
16th century. Knotted wool
$62\frac{1}{2} \times 137\frac{3}{4}$ in (159 × 350 cm)

53

Anatolia

Like the previous example, this carpet also features the typical star-shaped medallion on a brilliant red background. The well developed design of the border gives this piece its special charm. It has all the characteristics of a true 18th century carpet: brilliant colours, rich in contrast, (including the use of a clear yellow), soft, silky wool, and a flexible foundation which feels smooth to the touch. These carpets have been much copied during the last 100 years so care should be taken to check for the characteristics mentioned above. If the colour of the wool is dull, the backing stiff and the wool feels brittle, call in the advice of an expert.

Anatolia. Star Ushak
About 1700. Knotted wool. Private collection, Milan
$47\frac{1}{4} \times 77$ in (120 × 195 cm)

Anatolia

The carpet weavers of the Konya region have produced an astonishing number of different designs, which constantly provide fresh surprises for connoisseur and collector. The little carpet opposite is one of the rarest pieces of which only one other example (in the Budapest Museum) is so far known to exist. Apparently the carpet was originally intended for use as a runner and was later shortened by sewing the two halves together side by side. The extra piece of border was used to finish off the carpet. Oddly enough, the same procedure was adopted with the one in the Budapest Museum. Although the border would seem to indicate a 17th century Ushak carpet, the central pattern, with its tulips, delphiniums and other plants—often growing out of vases—is more typical of Konya work. The attractive design of the central panel is a real tribute to the imagination of its creator.

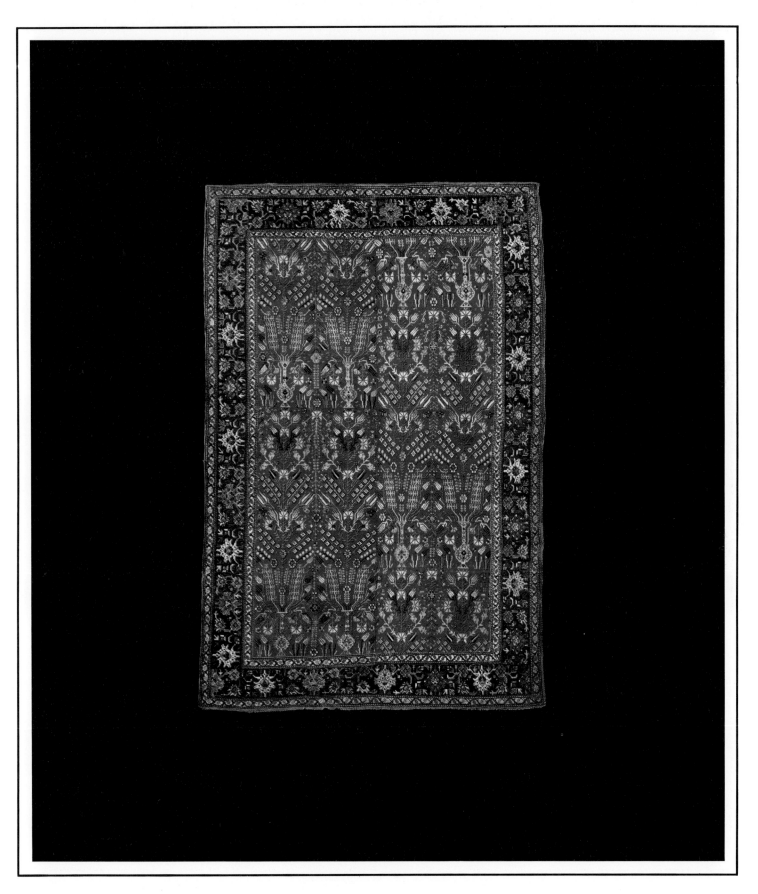

Anatolia. Konya region
17th–18th century. Knotted wool
$75\frac{1}{4} \times 113\frac{3}{4}$ in (190 × 287 cm)

Anatolia

From the 16th century to the beginning of the 18th, prayer rugs were made in Anatolia for export to Transylvania (called in German *Siebenbürgen*), where they can still be seen today, decorating the walls of the churches. The name of the sponsor was sometimes worked into the *kilim* (edging). These carpets, generally called 'Transylvanians' by collectors and dealers, have so far not been easy to identify accurately. Some can be placed in Konya, Melas, Ushak or Bergama because of their design and structure. Others, however, like the one shown opposite, still defy identification. It was most probably woven in the Ushak region. The design of the main border gives a good indication of its age. Early examples, such as this one which probably dates back to the 16th century, show a star decoration between each cartouche. In later pieces the stars disappear and the cartouches are continuous (see page 63). Nearly all the rugs are the same size and have a prayer niche on one side which, in some carpets, has been extended to make a double niche. Occasionally this device has also been repeated in the lower half of the carpet. The oldest rugs are vivid in colour, with light colours predominating. Collectors should note that authentic examples of this type of carpet have a yellow or green woollen warp. In the famous McMullan Collection, New York, there is a carpet which is exactly the same in colour and design as the one opposite except that it has a double niche.

Anatolia. Transylvanian carpet
About 1600. Knotted wool. Private collection, Bergisch-Gladbach
$47\frac{1}{4} \times 60\frac{1}{4}$ in (120×153 cm)

Anatolia

In contrast to the previous carpet, the colour and design of this one place it in the 17th century. The design of the central panel is simpler and there is a double niche. Nevertheless, cartouches and stars still alternate in the border. The crenellated design on the inner and outer bands of the border on the previous carpet has changed: while the outer band still displays the pattern of crenellations, the inner one now has the leaf-wave tendrils characteristic of 17th century carpets. The colours in the central panel give this Transylvanian carpet a greater value for collectors.

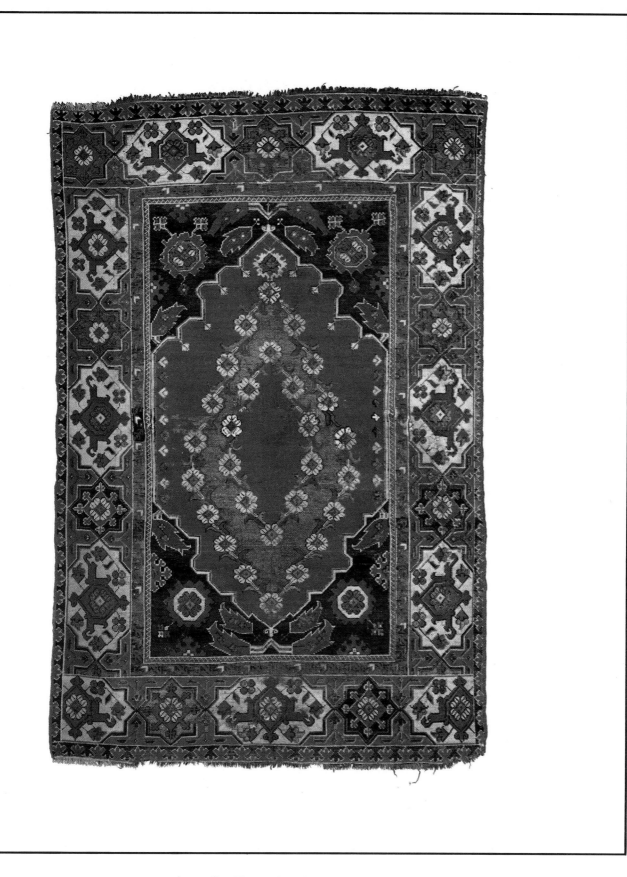

Anatolia. Transylvanian carpet
17th century. Knotted wool. Private collection, Hamburg
$41\frac{3}{4} \times 65$ in (108 $\times$ 165 cm)

Anatolia

A comparison of this carpet with those on pages 59 and 61 clearly shows the development in the design. The stars have been omitted from the main border and both the inner and outer bands have a reciprocal pattern of crenellated shapes whereas the carpet on page 59 still displays the authentic crenellations. The central panel, too, has lost the severity of its design: it conveys a more random, less organic impression. All the same, both the colours and the structure place this carpet in the 17th century. Unfortunately a dealer who was in possession of the carpet for a time and who wished to give it a more 'correct' appearance, removed the yellow *kilim* (the carpet is shown complete in plate 48 of the Bernheimer Collection catalogue). This regrettable act should teach collectors the value of keeping as much as possible of the original carpet. Outer borders should never be removed or a tattered *kilim* cut off. After all, both bear witness to the carpet's age and original appearance.

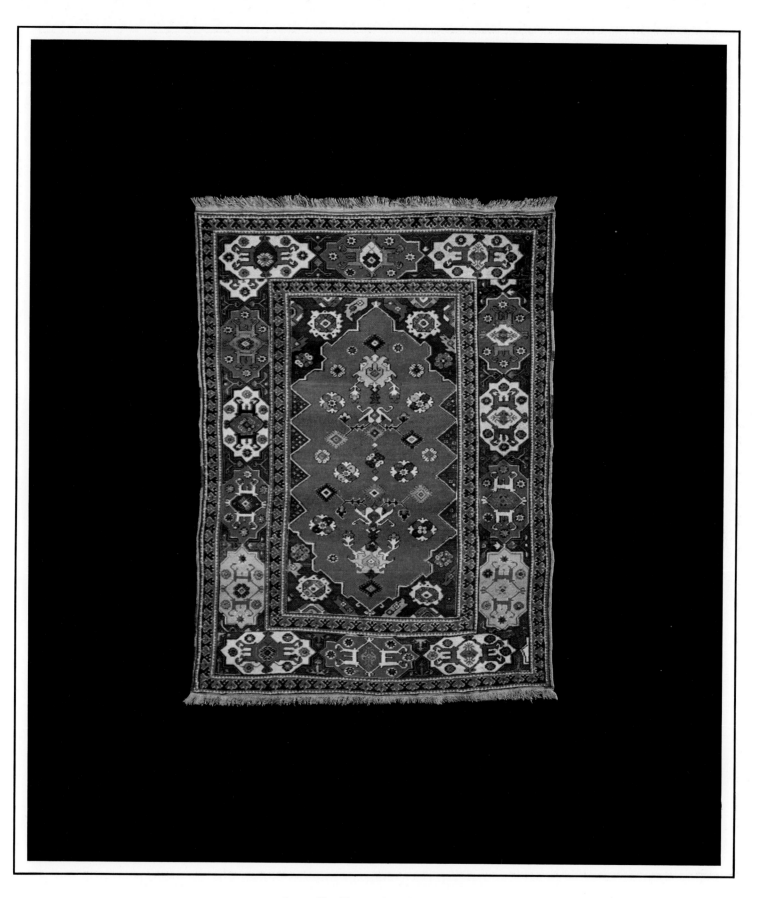

Anatolia. Transylvanian carpet
17th century. Knotted wool. Formerly in Bernheimer Collection
47 × 63¾ in (119 × 162 cm)

Anatolia

The relationship with the 'Transylvanian' carpets is obvious. In this one, too, there is a double niche in the central panel. The colours used, and their juxtaposition, are very similar to those in the Transylvanian carpet on page 59, whilst the design of the border unmistakably places it in the Melas region. Of considerable significance, here, is the careful handling of the corner decoration. In these carpets, with their flamboyant border design of flowers, the corners are rarely successful. The design is often abruptly interrupted and then forced home. This carpet can therefore be regarded as an especially beautiful early piece, dating from about 1700. In this case the dealer was sensible enough to leave the damaged *kilim* alone.

Anatolia. Melas region
About 1700. Private collection, Hamburg
$49\frac{1}{4} \times 62\frac{1}{4}$ in (125×158 cm)

Anatolia

Ladik carpets are among the most sought-after collectors' items, especially those dating from the 16th and 17th centuries which most faithfully reflect the oriental style of architecture in the design of their central panel. The border, with its rosettes, also points to this date of origin. A row of tulips in the upper part of the carpet seems to have been characteristic of most carpets knotted in the Ladik region. No other carpet can surpass the Ladik for the brilliance of its colours. Apart from a glowing red and a deep, sometimes almost turquoise, blue, it is the yellow which, above all, dominates the carpet with its intensity.

Anatolia. Column Ladik
17th century. Knotted wool. Private collection, Murnau
$40\frac{1}{4} \times 59\frac{3}{4}$ in (102 × 152 cm)

Anatolia

Also of 17th century origin, but later in date than the preceding carpet, this piece clearly shows the change in style. The architecture of the pillars in the central panel is simplified and, instead of complicated rosettes, the border is composed of cartouches containing a cruciform design. This carpet, with its simpler construction, also creates a very attractive impression.

There can be no denying its similarity to the Transylvanian carpets. Indeed a number of these carpets too can be found in the Transylvanian churches.

Anatolia. Ladik region
17th century. Knotted wool. Private collection, Hamburg
$54\frac{1}{4} \times 67$ in (138 × 170 cm)

Anatolia

At the beginning of the 18th century the style of the Ladik carpets changed decisively. Instead of the complicated columns, intended to represent the architecture of a mosque, a staggered, stylized prayer niche took its place. However the tulip pattern in the upper part of the central panel remained. The border also changed. Rosettes and tulips combined to form a kind of wavy tendril. Of these carpets, which are renowned for the brilliance of their colours, a comparatively large number has survived. In contrast to the rugs of earlier centuries, the basic structure is stiffer and more tightly packed, and the colours in the prayer niche are more varied. Apart from the normal red and blue niches, white and green ones can also be seen. In the Ewgaf Museum, Istanbul, there are some dated Ladiks. The most attractive and interesting carpets of this kind were made between 1750 and 1780.

Anatolia. Ladik region
18th century. Knotted wool. Private collection, Hamburg
41 × 65 in (104 × 165 cm)

Anatolia

Towards the end of the 18th and beginning of the 19th century, the design of the Ladik carpets declined still further. The architecture, which, in 16th and 17th century rugs was still clearly recognizable, became abstract, to form a triple-beam design. In addition, the row of tulips, which had divided the central panel, became an ornamentation which only contained fragments of tulips. The main border was reduced to a simple row of rosettes.

Nevertheless there is a great charm about these carpets, partly due to the harmony and range of their colours. Carpets like this were being woven well into the 19th century, admittedly with an even simpler design until at last only three beams were left in a plain-coloured central panel.

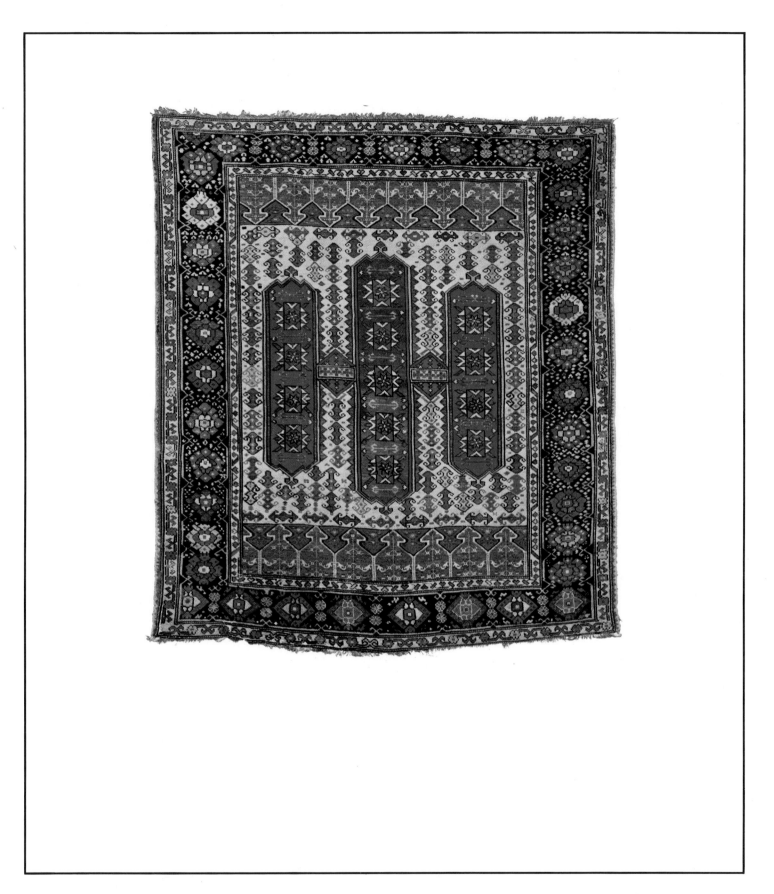

Anatolia. Ladik region
Early 19th century. Knotted wool. Private collection, Hamburg
$69\frac{1}{4} \times 76\frac{3}{4}$ in (176 × 195 cm)

Anatolia

Ladik carpets with a white background, that is, those which have a basically white *mihrab*, are very rare; how much rarer, therefore, is a carpet like this one which, at the earliest, could have come from Konya and in which the whole inner panel has a white background covered with the kind of repeating pattern normally only found in the border (see the next carpet). The enchanting combination of colours and rosettes with floral decorations gives the carpet an irresistible charm. The main border is in contrast with its blue background and unusual, superbly coloured flower-tendril pattern. The first-class condition of this carpet is shown by the gleaming wool and basic weave that are such a feature of Konya carpets.

Anatolia. Ladik. Konya region
18th century. Knotted wool. Kinebanian Collection, Amsterdam
59 × 76¾ in (150 × 195 cm)

Anatolia

Konya carpets have a certain natural relationship with those from the neighbouring Ladik region. Thus this one has the row of tulips above its *mihrab* typical of Ladik carpets. However, both the range of colours and coarser weave on the softer basic structure point to Konya as its place of origin. As so often with carpets from this region, the eye is gladdened by the beautiful colour contrasts which have maintained their brilliance for more than a century.

Anatolia. Konya
19th century. Knotted wool
$47\frac{1}{2} \times 61\frac{3}{4}$ in (121 × 157 cm)

Anatolia

The arrangement of three star-shaped medallions, followed by a partially completed one, shows that a continuous pattern was intended. This is in the Islamic philosophical tradition and reflects a desire to give expression to a sense of the infinite even in carpets. Note the subtle way in which the lower part of the border is distinguished from the upper. Many carpets of this period still look primitive and can be compared with nomadic ones.

Anatolia. Konya
19th century. Knotted wool
$41\frac{1}{4} \times 100$ in (105×254 cm)

Anatolia

Nomadic Yürük rugs have many features in common with those from the Bergama regions. However, the colours of the wool reveal considerable differences. Dark colours predominate, in particular a deep brown, adorned with a highly individual green geometric pattern. The border in the one opposite is reminiscent of the Turkoman carpets of the Ogurdjals (see Schürmann: *Central Asian Rugs*). It can therefore be regarded as proof that in ancient times the Turkoman tribes penetrated Asia Minor and made use of their ancient patterns in Anatolia. The silky gleam of the comparatively long pile is, as always, a distinguishing mark of Yürük carpets.

Anatolia. Yürük
19th century. Knotted wool
$58\frac{1}{2} \times 83\frac{1}{2}$ in (148 × 212 cm)

79

Anatolia

It is rare for collectors to find a dated carpet—all the more exciting, then, to find one with such an unusual design as well. Whereas the central panel is decorated with a severely geometric pattern reminiscent of Turkish *güls*, the border contains the typical Anatolian ornamentation of the Ghiordes rugs. The variety of design and richness of colour contrasts are once again marvellous to behold. Surely there cannot be another carpet anything like it.

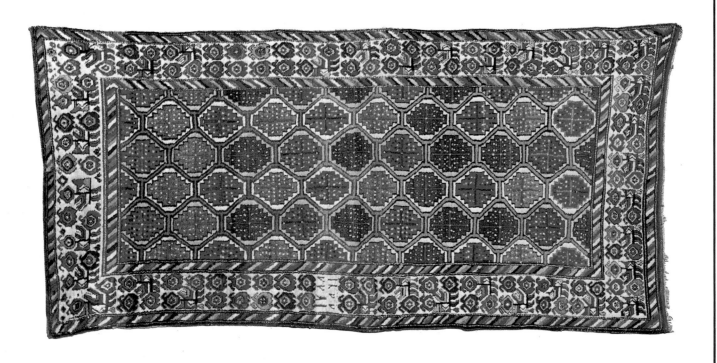

Anatolia. Yürük
Dated 1288 by Islamic chronology (1872 by our reckoning)
59 × 125¼ in (150 × 318 cm)

80

Anatolia

The carpets woven by the nomadic craftsmen of Yürük are among the most imaginative expressions of Anatolian art. They rely less on the use of a particular design or arrangement, and rather more on a restricted range of colour. An orangey-red predominates and is often used in conjunction with large areas of brown native wool. The structure of these rugs is unmistakable. Notice the smooth, round knots visible on the back, the softness of the wool and the long pile. Normally the design on a long-piled rug tends to become indistinct and vague. This does not happen with Yürük rugs as they are so much more finely knotted than the other Anatolian carpets.

Collectors should not be put off by the fact that they are not rectangular in shape. It could almost be regarded as characteristic of Yürük rugs that they are crooked or have one side longer than the other.

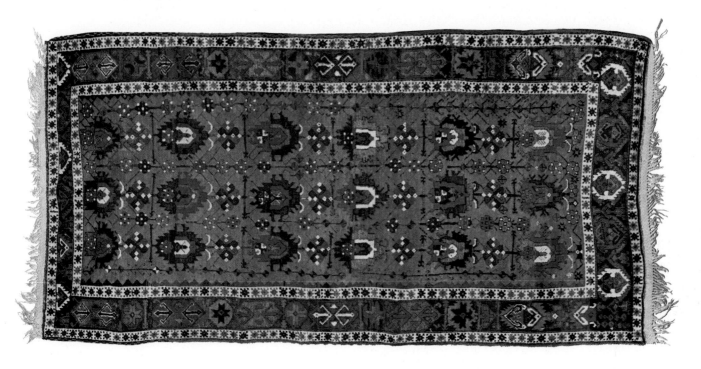

Anatolia. Yürük
19th century. Knotted wool. Private collection, Hamburg
$52\frac{3}{4} \times 104\frac{1}{4}$ in (134 × 265 cm)

Anatolia

Judging from its design, this carpet could easily have come from several different districts in Anatolia. It displays motifs typical of Mujur carpets, a border design as used in the Ushak region, and a Bergama pattern for the central panel. Because of its structure, however— the long pile, soft wool and range of colours—it must be classified as coming from Yürük. No doubt the craftsmen of Yürük often borrowed motifs from the designs of their neighbours.

Anatolia. Yürük
About 1800. Knotted wool. Private collection, Hamburg
$52\frac{3}{4} \times 68\frac{3}{4}$ in (134 × 175 cm)

Anatolia

From the end of the 18th century until about 1870 the most strikingly beautiful carpets were woven in the Melas district. The fine, silky wool was not the least of their charms. The red, yellow and blue in the carpet opposite harmonizes perfectly. A double border surrounds a central panel which may possibly contain a stylized version of the tree of life.

Some collectors may have noticed that there is often a change of colours in the central panel of Melas carpets, the upper half being worked in a different tone from the lower. An explanation for this, put forward in Armenia, was that the different tones were meant to represent day and night. Another characteristic of Melas carpets is that the ornamentation of the prayer arch is often freely imaginative rather than tied to a religious convention.

Anatolia. Melas
First half of 19th century. Knotted wool. Private collection, Hamburg
$39\frac{3}{4} \times 61\frac{1}{4}$ in (100 × 156 cm)

Anatolia

There are hundreds of carpets which, like the one opposite with its red, furled prayer arch on a white background, demonstrate a further development of the classical 17th/18th century design. The border becomes wider and is filled with more varied patterns. Rosettes or flowers, surrounded by spear-shaped leaves, are shown in a medley of ornaments, the ensemble forming a most delightful picture.

When considering Melas rugs—and especially those of Mujur or other Anatolian types of design—collectors should make sure that a cochineal shade is present in the knotted surface. The colour can range from a deep, purple brown to the very faintest tint of violet. It is evidence that the carpet is comparatively old—dating from before 1870 at the very latest. Wool that is dyed cochineal tends to fade more on the outer end of the tuft of wool than on the part that is knotted. Only small areas were generally worked in this colour because the dye was so expensive.

Anatolia. Melas
First half of 19th century. Knotted wool. Private collection, Hamburg
$55\frac{1}{4} \times 63\frac{3}{4}$ in (140 × 162 cm)

Anatolia

Between 1820 and 1860 carpets were made in Anatolia—especially in the Melas and Ghiordes regions—whose design reflects the strong influence of European taste. The carpet opposite is a typical example of this genre and was probably intended for the French market. The subdued colours and almost representational floral design have pushed the oriental character into the background. These carpets have considerable appeal. They admirably suit rooms with appropriate furniture—especially pieces from the early 19th century.

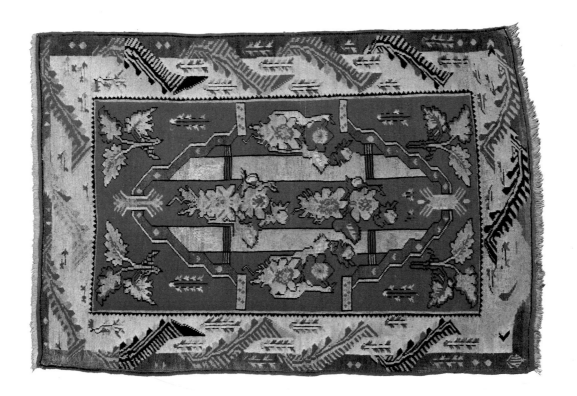

Anatolia. Melas
First half of 19th century. Knotted wool
$33 \times 49\frac{1}{4}$ in (84×125 cm)

Anatolia

Carpets knotted in Mujur are distinguished by their unusual design and unique combination of colours. Very often there is a row of semi-hexagons filled with floral shapes at each end of the rug. However the magnificent colours and the use of cochineal over large areas are more important as indications of origin. Carpets displaying a horizontal row of prayer arches are extremely rare.

Anatolia. Mujur
First half of 19th century. Knotted wool. Private collection, Graz
$42\frac{1}{4} \times 59\frac{3}{4}$ in (107 × 152 cm)

Anatolia

This carpet must be one of the most beautiful Mujurs for colour, construction and design. It once formed part of the famous Mavrogordato collection in the Pera Palace, Istanbul.

Here, too, the corners above the unusual prayer arch are worked in a wonderful cochineal wool. The colour changes in the border of leaf shapes on a golden-yellow background bear witness to the imagination and astonishing versatility of the weaver. Unfortunately only a few Mujurs of this quality have survived.

Anatolia. Mujur
About 1800. Knotted wool. Private collection, Uitikon, Switzerland
$42\frac{1}{2} \times 52$ in (108 $\times$ 132 cm)

Anatolia

The weavers of Bergama have produced a considerable number of rugs known as rustic carpets. In view of this description, the delicate artistry of the craftsman comes as something of a surprise. The carpets are almost without exception fairly coarsely woven. They have a short pile made of tough, silky wool, which enables the colours to stand out in rich contrast. Unlike other Anatolian carpets, the background colour is frequently green. There are often green or blue *kilims*, too, as well as the more usual red ones. There are a great many of these beautiful carpets in the McMullan Collection, New York. Their striking design and colouring make them especially attractive to collectors.

A special point of interest in the carpet opposite is the border. It includes bands of clouds in geometric and abstract form which are unquestionably borrowed from more explicit and elegant 16th century prototypes.

A characteristic of nearly all Bergama carpets is that the red dye used for the backgrounds gradually tended to rot the wool. As a result, the surface of the carpets developed a relief appearance.

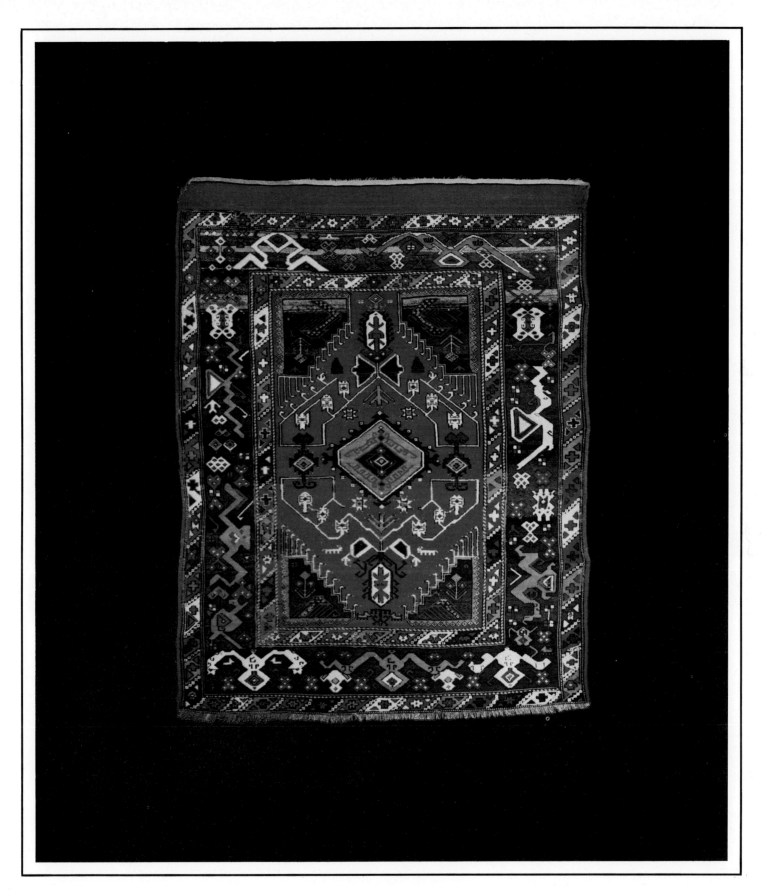

Anatolia. Bergama
18th century. Knotted wool
69 × 82¼ in (175 × 208 cm)

91

Anatolia

This carpet can be regarded as the pearl of oriental craftsmanship. The economy of its design, and the unusual use of broken-up colours on a natural-toned, camelhair background show that it was made by a real artist. A very similar rug is in the Metropolitan Museum, New York.

Anatolia. Bergama
About 1800. Knotted wool. Private collection, Graz
$39\frac{3}{4} \times 50$ in (101 × 127 cm)

Anatolia

The carpets of the Dosemealtai are generally almost square; small rugs are preferred although there are also some which are as large as $70\frac{3}{4} \times 86\frac{1}{2}$ in (180 × 220 cm). Whereas the bigger pieces are robustly primitive in colour and design, the smaller carpets reflect a rare elegance considering their nomadic and rustic origin. The rug below looks as if it has been knotted on a green background. This type of rug is encountered more often in the Dosemealtai region than in other parts of Anatolia.

Anatolia. Dosemealtai
First half of 19th century. Knotted wool. Private collection, Hamburg
$47\frac{1}{4} \times 50\frac{1}{2}$ in (120 × 128 cm)

Anatolia

It is rare for a collector to come across a carpet which has such a powerful colour and design. Two immense polygons in black and dark blue dominate the central panel. They are surrounded by triangles filled with a hook-shaped pattern. The comparatively narrow border with its archaic S-forms emphasizes the age of the carpet. Although few colours were used, the effect is surprisingly striking. The pattern is reminiscent of that in the rugs often seen lying at the feet of the Madonna in pictures painted by Van Eyck and his pupils.

Anatolia. Bergama
About 1800. Knotted wool
56 × 72 in (142 × 183 cm)

Anatolia

What a contrast—both in colour and design—to the previous carpet! Although the central panel of both has two big polygons and hook-filled triangles, in this version, made about fifty to a hundred years later, the colours have become more subdued and the naturalistic strength of the earlier carpet has become more refined, perhaps even degenerate. Nevertheless the carpet is typical of its time. The polygons dominating the central panel are reminiscent of the Lesghi stars on Caucasian rugs. The impeccable condition of this carpet is remarkable.

Anatolia. Bergama
About 1850. Knotted wool
$65\frac{3}{4} \times 86\frac{3}{4}$ in (167 × 220 cm)

97

Anatolia

Ghiordes and Kula rugs have always been in great demand. The beautiful harmony of their colours plus the charm of their design captivates many collectors.

In Ghiordes, as in all places where carpets are made, there are great differences in quality and artistic worth. The rug opposite is outstanding for its wealth of ornamentation and daring colour contrasts. It is also rare to find carpets more than 59 in (150 cm) wide. This earlier piece must have stood out from the mass of Ghiordes and Kula rugs as a highly desirable object even 100 years ago.

Anatolia. Ghiordes
Early 19th century. Knotted wool
61 × 109 in (155 × 208 cm)

Anatolia

A considerable number of carpets—almost all of them prayer rugs —were woven in the Ghiordes/Kula regions during the 19th century. They were very popular and exported in their thousands. Of these, the rugs, reflecting a French influence which tried to satisfy both oriental and European taste in their colour and design, form a sub-group. Some people may reject these rugs for aesthetic reasons; nevertheless, no one can deny that even under European influence attractive, elegant carpets were made during the first half of the 19th century.

Anatolia. Ghiordes
About 1820. Knotted wool. Private collection, Hamburg
$54\frac{1}{4} \times 74\frac{3}{4}$ in (138 × 190 cm)

101

Anatolia

This handsome carpet vividly demonstrates what happens when a design is not carried out accurately. Although the colour scheme unmistakably places the carpet in Melas, the design is imprecise, haphazard and degenerate. Cotton was used for the white areas. In fact, it is incredible that in spite of so many faults of accuracy and style it should seem so much more charming than it really is. Perhaps it is just this accidental quality which is the reason for its attraction.

Anatolia. Melas
19th century. Knotted wool
$28\frac{3}{4} \times 41$ in (73×104 cm)

Anatolia

At the end of the 19th century, a great many carpets were woven for export and home consumption in Anatolia. The colours gradually became more garish and the design degenerated. Dealers began to use the collective name 'Anatolian' for any rugs which no longer bore any local characteristics. This marked the start of a general decline which was to lead to the introduction of aniline dyes and the end of Anatolian carpets so far as collectors were concerned.

Anatolia. Probably Kishehir
19th century. Knotted wool
$47\frac{1}{4} \times 56\frac{3}{4}$ in (120 × 144 cm)

Anatolia

For a long time, the oriental, purely woven carpet was regarded as of secondary importance by collectors and was not highly regarded. This is a pity as it is often the *kilim* which represents the true local craftsmanship. The technique of weaving and work at the loom, particularly where pentahedral geometric forms were employed, permitted the use of other patterns. Perhaps the reason they were ignored by collectors was that there was so little use for them in a European home. It is only quite recently that collectors have begun to take more notice of them, perhaps because old, knotted carpets are becoming more difficult to acquire. Curiously enough, interest in *kilims* began in the United States, though meanwhile they have also achieved a following in Europe. They can still be acquired comparatively cheaply. Collectors who cannot afford to buy a knotted carpet should certainly consider woven ones. These beautiful, richly coloured carpets are also examples of truly imaginative skill.

Anatolia. *Kilim*
19th century. Woven wool. Private collection, Hahnwald, near Cologne
43 × 57½ in (109 × 146 cm)

105

Egypt

The carpets made by the Mamelukes are so strikingly individual that they can never be confused with any other oriental carpet. Many of those made before the Osman conquest are only in three colours—red, blue and a yellowish green. A silvery haze lies over all early pieces, due to the fineness of the wool used.

The central panel is filled with an astonishing variety of imaginative ornaments. Many of these rare carpets look similar at first glance. It is only after close scrutiny that the considerable differences in design become apparent, these having been concealed, to some extent, by the economical use of colours. In contrast, the border is composed of rounded cartouches against a background of the finest leaf tendrils.

A feature of these carpets is the basic foundation in which sometimes the warp and sometimes the weft are brown or green. Some carpets were probably also knotted with silk for one of these—perhaps the most beautiful carpet in the world—is at present in the Museum for Applied Arts in Vienna.

Egypt. Mameluke carpet
About 1500. Knotted wool
$51\frac{1}{4} \times 69$ in (130×175 cm)

Egypt

Until the Osmans conquered Egypt, that country had a flourishing carpet industry which reached its peak during the days of the Mamelukes. Until about the middle of the 16th century, the rugs woven by Mamelukes could compete for beauty and intricacy of design with any Persian carpet of the Shah-Abbas era. One of the most beautiful carpets in the world is the silky Mameluke carpet in the Museum of Applied Arts in Vienna. A characteristic of Mameluke carpets is that they restrict themselves to only a few colours: red, green, turquoise and yellow. The weft is always green, the wool is fine, silky and gleaming. The design is a masterpiece of geometric composition.

After the Osman conquest, although the colours, wool and structure of the carpets remained the same, the design changed. Flowers, tendrils and leaves replaced a geometric arrangement. The carpet opposite is a classical example of the earliest masterpieces woven by Egyptian craftsmen under Osman rule.

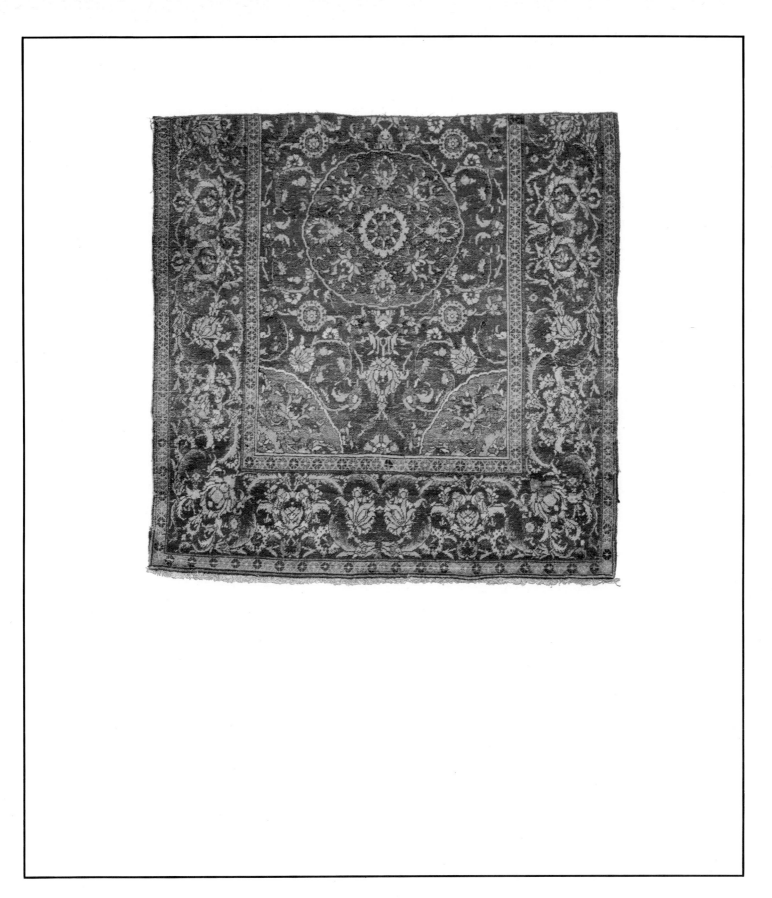

Egypt. Osman carpet
About 1600. Knotted wool
$52\frac{1}{2} \times 54\frac{1}{4}$ in (133 × 138 cm) (Fragment)

Persia

The picture opposite shows a fragment of a carpet which was manufactured at court and which was originally double the length. Knotted on a silken warp, it reproduces animals, flowers and bands of clouds with the utmost artistic skill. The design of the bottle-green border is restricted to flowers and leaf tendrils and is in contrast to the red background. Carpets of this type are among the most coveted examples of the Persian craft. Thanks to a strange chance, the other half of the carpet has also been found. It is in a private collection in Switzerland.

Persia. Kashan
Mid 16th century. Knotted wool. Museum of Art and Weaving, Hamburg
$73\frac{1}{4} \times 127\frac{3}{4}$ in (186 × 310 cm). (Fragment)

111

Persia

A great many impressive carpets were made in north-west Persia during the 18th century. They often display both Persian and Caucasian decorations. Typically Persian palm leaves alternate with the forked tendrils of Caucasian Karagashli rugs. The Persian design, with its elegant lines, appears stiff and geometric here. The craftsman who made this rug used a particularly wide range of colours, a wealth of different tones being combined with a most unusual green. They stand out like relief on the camel-coloured background. The imagination shown by these Kurdish tribes is a constant source of admiration.

Persia. North-west Persian carpet
About 1800. Knotted wool
$66\frac{1}{2} \times 129$ in (169 × 328 cm)

Persia

In eastern Persia during the 16th and 17th centuries, there were workshops which produced carpets with accurately worked floral designs, usually on a red background. Since a great many such carpets seem to have been made, and they bore a certain resemblance to those of Ispahan, they were often wrongly described as 'Ispahan' or 'Indo-Ispahan'.

In the early pieces, the design of the central panel, which is very much more complicated than would appear at first sight, possesses a beguiling loveliness and proportion. Later the design degenerated considerably and the colours were no longer so carefully chosen. The fragment opposite, which represents little more than half the carpet, belongs to the earlier period. This can be seen by the bottle-green border which, with its carefully drawn pattern of flowers and arabesques, stands out so well from the background red of the central panel. A glance at the backing will help to distinguish this group of Herat carpets from those which were really made in Ispahan or by the Moghuls in India. In genuine Ispahans, the warp and weft threads lie close together and this gives the carpets a certain density and inflexibility. Those made in India have a looser weave with a short pile and are rather granular to the touch. The construction of the Herat carpets lies somewhere in between these two extremes. They are of medium density, with a short pile and feel comparatively soft in the hand. The wool of the knots is softer and more silky than the dry, somewhat brittle wool of their Indian counterparts.

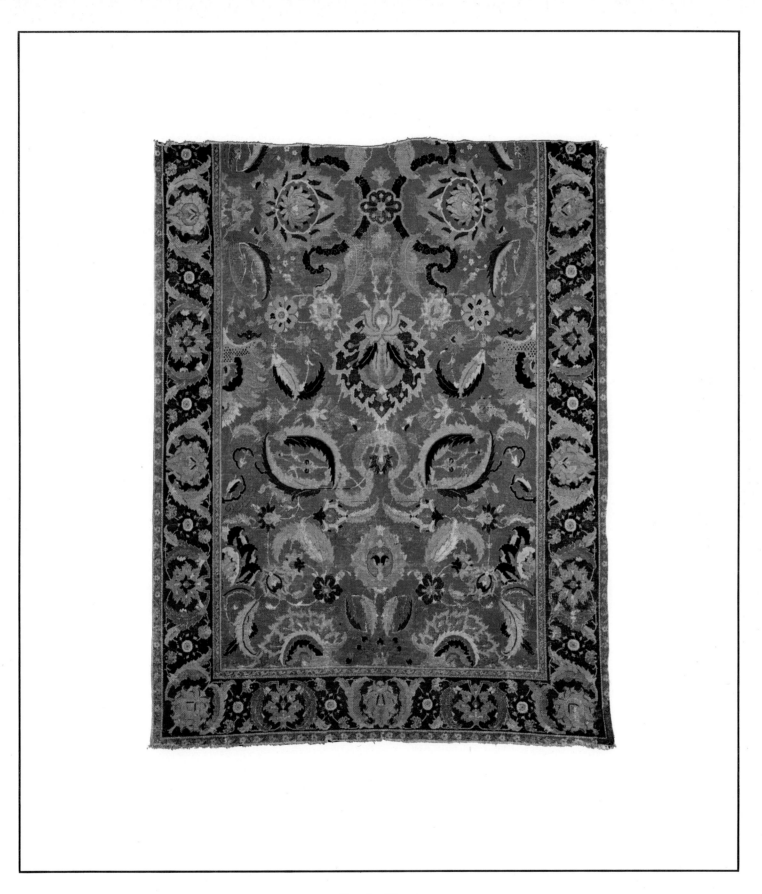

Persia. Herat
17th century. Knotted wool. Formerly in the A. Kann Collection, Paris
$69\frac{3}{4} \times 89\frac{1}{4}$ in (177×227 cm)

Persia

All that is best in Persian ornamentation and colour composition is united in this carpet. The extended design of the basic composition makes an almost gothic impression. The mass of floral motifs is interrupted by large scale tendrils. The work in the border is reminiscent of the artistic quality found in the best 15th and 16th century north Persian rugs. When the rug opposite was being made, a workshop in Herez began to make silk carpets which can be classed among the most beautiful of the 18th century. They can be recognized by their light colouring and a particular shade of rust-red, as well as the unusually fine, flexible texture of their knotting.

Persia. Ispahan
18th century. Knotted silk
$50\frac{1}{2} \times 93\frac{1}{2}$ in (128 × 238 cm)

Persia

The most obvious characteristic of carpets from Bijar is their remarkably dense, heavy backing. As a result the carpets are hard to fold and there is a danger of breaking the weft threads, whether or not there has been any rotting. This makes the delicacy of the design in the rug opposite all the more surprising. The pattern is derived from the classical garden rugs.

Persia. Bijar
Early 19th century. Knotted wool
$63\frac{3}{4} \times 88\frac{3}{4}$ in (162 $\times$ 225 cm)

Persia

There are perhaps half a dozen big silk carpets which appear to come from the same manufacturer and to be very similar in structure. To these belongs the famous Viennese hunting carpet. There was a complete carpet in a Polish collection, the counterpart of the fragment pictured right, with a sea-green central panel. It must have been a very beautifully coloured piece. The fragment opposite, which only consists of skilfully pieced together parts of border, conveys some impression of the nobility and elegance of the carpet.

Persia. Kashan
Mid 16th century. Knotted silk. Museum of Art and Weaving, Hamburg
$54\frac{1}{4} \times 101\frac{1}{2}$ in (138 × 258 cm). (Fragment)

Persia

There has always been a great demand for Senneh rugs, with their short pile, the extremely fine texture of their knotting and their carefully graded colour schemes. The motif which is most often used is a boteh-flower, which usually extends over the whole carpet. An arrangement of narrow strips, ranged side by side in alternate colours, as in the carpet opposite, is extremely rare.

Apart from the true Sennehs, there are the Sennehs from Kurdistan of recent manufacture, and Malahir carpets, both of which are often wrongly offered for sale as Sennehs. Collectors should note that the Sennehs from Kurdistan have a much coarser, thicker backing. The wool is drier and the colours look duller. Malahir carpets, on the other hand, have a much smoother construction and the range of colours includes a particular light red which often tends to run. True Senneh carpets have a coarse, grainy feel, with a fine weave and round knots. The wool is silky and makes the colours gleam with life.

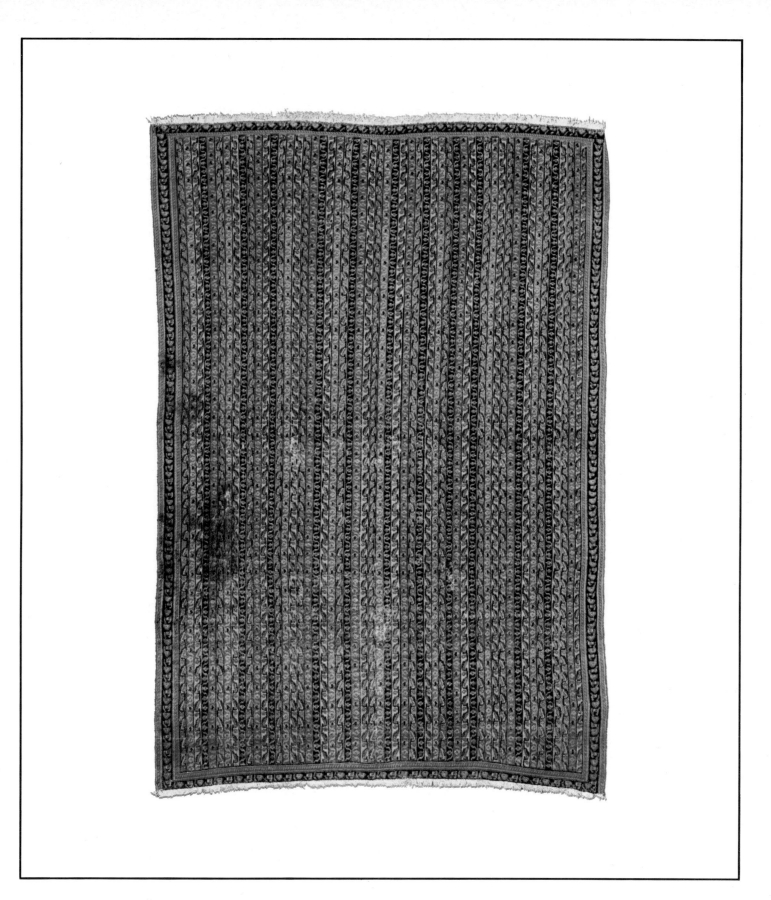

Persia. Senneh
Early 19th century. Knotted wool
$51\frac{1}{2} \times 73\frac{1}{2}$ in (131 × 187 cm)

Persia

A characteristic of Karadjah carpets has always been a geometrication of the Persian line. The influence of the Caucasus has made itself felt. The carpet shown here is typical. The weeping willows at the foot of the prayer arch are finished off at right angles; the cypresses seem to be covered with hooks; the tree of life resembles a child's drawing of a Christmas tree. The central panel above the *mihrab* provides a sharp contrast with its pattern resembling the tiles of a Persian mosque. The plain border gives the stimulating pattern in the central panel a calm frame.

This rug is clear proof that even at the beginning of the 19th century beautiful carpets were still being made in northern Persia.

Persia. Karadjah
Early 19th century. Knotted wool
51 × 72 in (130 × 183 cm)

123

Persia

In old Herez rugs there are often arabesques with the heads of dragons or other imaginary beasts. The carpet in the picture shows a Caucasian influence and reproduces archaic dragons not just on the camelhair background of its central panel but also in the blue corners of the design. The classical format, too—at least twice as long as it is broad—is evidence for the great age of this unusual collectors' piece.

The economy of the geometrical design surrounded by large monochrome areas—usually white, light blue or camelhair—always excites admiration. In addition, the tough wool used makes them one of the most hardwearing of the oriental rugs.

Persia. Herez
About 1800. Knotted wool
$51\frac{1}{2} \times 108\frac{1}{2}$ in (130 × 275 cm)

Persia

A later piece than the one on the previous page, the carpet opposite also features the characteristics of Herez work: pentahedral division, economy of ornamentation and glowing colours rich in contrast. It is extremely rare for Herez carpets to be so small. Usually they exceed 100 × 150 in (300 × 400 cm).

Persia. Herez
19th century. Knotted wool
$54\frac{3}{4} \times 67\frac{3}{4}$ in (139 × 172 cm)

Persia

The Kashgai of Southern Persia have always been noted for combining a fine texture of knotting and silky wool with a graceful pattern. One of the loveliest Kashgai rugs this author has ever seen is the Shiraz opposite with its white background and design glorifying the rose of Shiraz lauded so often by the Persian poets. The elegance of design, accuracy of line and careful choice of colours make this carpet a masterpiece of Kashgai craft. That the carpet has been preserved in perfect condition increases its value to collectors.

Persia. Kashgai
Early 19th century. Knotted wool
$51\frac{1}{2} \times 93\frac{1}{4}$ in (131 × 238 cm)

129

Persia

What has just been said about the preceding carpet can be repeated for this little gem of a Persian rug. The charm lies in the contrast between the winged border and the completely plain blue central panel. Considering that in the orient an undecorated panel was regarded as a sign of extraordinary extravagance, this carpet must have been a most unusual and costly object even at the time when it was made.

Persia. Kashgai
Early 19th century. Knotted wool
$33\frac{1}{2} \times 52$ in (85 × 132 cm)

Persia

Forty years ago there were still many of these splendid carpets on the market. Their light colours and cheerful patterns charmed the eye. In addition, the texture of the knotting was extremely fine and the wool was both soft and hardwearing. In later pieces the dyeing was so badly carried out that a dark shadowy impression was produced overall which excluded these carpets from becoming collectors' pieces.

Persia. Kashgai
19th century. Knotted wool
$44\frac{3}{4} \times 72\frac{3}{4}$ in (114 × 185 cm)

Persia

Carpets with an all-over pattern are comparatively rare in the Shiraz region. Whilst in central and eastern Persia the Herati and Minekhani design is prevalent, i.e. flowers surrounded by lanceolate leaves, in southern Persia this design has undergone a change. During the 16th and 17th centuries it developed into the so-called vase pattern, and during the 19th century, as in this carpet, it consisted of rosettes in many different colours strewn over a central field to look like a piece of ground strewn with petals.

Not as finely knotted and not as unusual as the two preceding ones from this region, this rug nevertheless is still evidence of good taste and a harmonious choice of colours.

Persia. Kashgai
Mid 19th century. Knotted wool
$60\frac{1}{4} \times 105\frac{1}{2}$ in (153×268 cm)

Persia

The workshops in Sarouk seem to have been particularly busy
during the 19th century. An above average number of carefully
worked carpets of Sedjadeh format and room carpet size was
exported from that district. The design was restricted almost
exclusively to a central medallion composed of different planes of
colour. Only the big carpets have a pattern repeat. Common to all
of them, however, is a strong, cotton backing, short pile and an
exceptionally hardwearing quality. The soft, gleaming wool
which was used in the older carpets often caused them to be mis-
taken for Kashan rugs whose design is very similar. Collectors
should bear in mind that Sarouk carpets can generally be distinguished from those of Kashan by their blue cotton weft.

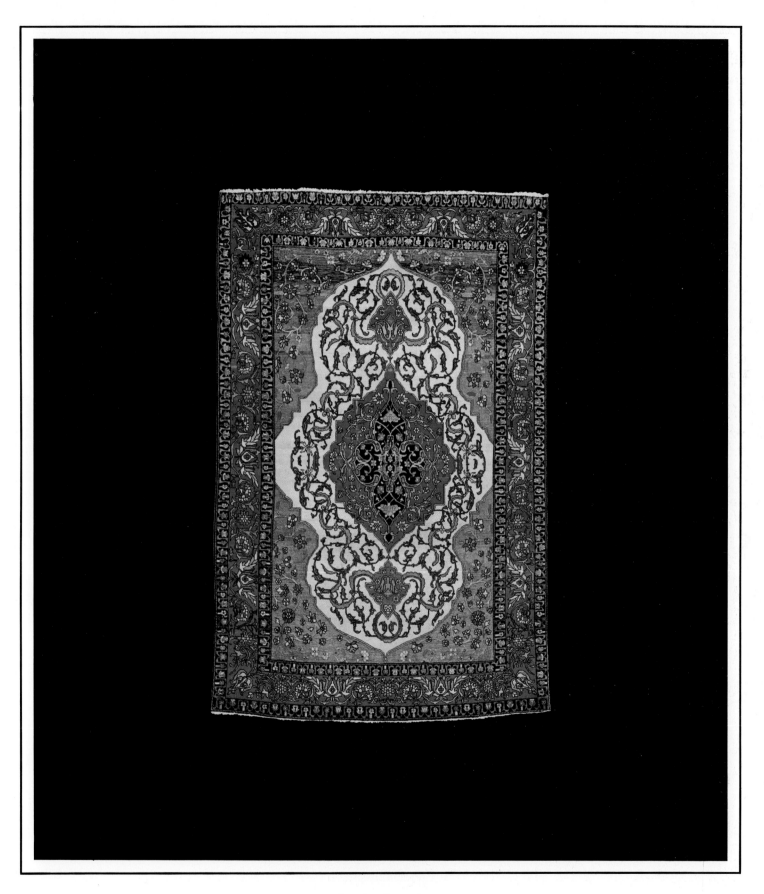

Persia. Sarouk
19th century. Knotted wool
52 × 81¾ in (132 × 208 cm)

Persia

Old Khorassan carpets are one of the few groups which are easy to identify. They are distinguished by a comparatively long, velvety, woollen pile which feels like fine ribbing on the back. The design often has a central medallion on a monochrome reflection, with corresponding designs in the corners of the central panel. Unfortunately, these carpets, whose delicate colours harmonize particularly well, deteriorate rapidly because of the soft wool from which they are made. Animals, especially hares, often feature in the early pieces. The boteh-flower was also often used as a repeating pattern in the smaller rugs.

Persia. Khorassan
19th century. Knotted wool
48 × 70 in (122 × 178 cm)

137

Caucasus

Only about half a dozen of these outstanding early 18th century carpets have survived. They can be found in the most famous museums of the world as well as in private collections like the Ballard or McMullan collections. Only the one which once belonged to Beghian has, like the one shown here, a foundation made of silk. It is a classical 17th–18th century Caucasian carpet, that is to say it displays a one-sided stepped pattern (for further details see *Caucasian Rugs* by the same author).

The charm of the carpet is not just in the elegance of design and colour and the filigree-like border, but in the sensation when handled. The very short pile, together with the silken warp, gives the rug the pliability of the finest silken cloth.

Caucasus. Shirvan
Mid-18th century. Knotted wool on a silken warp
$50\frac{1}{2} \times 114\frac{1}{4}$ in (128 × 290 cm)

139

Caucasus

If it were not for the typically Caucasian animal designs which are worked into one corner of the border, these carpets could also be classed as Persian of the post-classical period. It is rare for carpets of this shape to come from the Karabagh region. Generally they were at least twice as long as they were broad. Certainly the influence of Persia's neighbours can be seen here. The easiest way of identifying 17th and 18th century Karabagh carpets is by the presence of a particular bluish-red. It is a strong colour, which dominates the whole carpet, all the other colours becoming subsidiary to it.

Caucasus. Karabagh
17th century. Knotted wool
110 × 130 in (280 × 330 cm)

141

Caucasus

This carpet stands out from the mass of 18th and 19th century Shirvan carpets as something special. The extremely dense ornamentation is reminiscent of the silk embroideries on a linen backing which were also being made in the Caucasus at that time. (Some of these embroideries are shown in *Carpets of the Caucasus* by the same author.) It is hard to say whether the embroideries acted as models for the carpets or the other way round. In the Ewgaf Museum, Istanbul, there is a $78\frac{3}{4} \times 118$ in (200×300 cm) rug in which the design and colours exactly match an embroidery reproduced as plate 138 in the above book. Whatever the truth, the piece shown here is attractive because of the multitude of its ornamentation and the constant change of colour. It is one of those unusual pieces of which every collector can be proud.

Caucasus. Shirvan region
17th–18th century. Knotted wool
44 × 48 in (112 × 122 cm)

Caucasus

This carpet, one of the famous Mavrogordato Collection in the Pera Palace, Istanbul, is outstanding for the fine texture of the knotting, imaginative use of colours, well balanced design and perfect condition.

The Mughan region was originally inhabited by Tartars, noted for their skill in knotting. The unerring confidence with which these craftsmen made apparently clashing colour combinations harmonize is truly remarkable.

Caucasus. Mughan region
About 1800. Knotted wool. Private collection, Paris
$48\frac{1}{2} \times 102\frac{1}{2}$ in. (123×260 cm)

Caucasus

A characteristic of 18th-century Caucasian carpets is the one-sided ascending pattern of floral motifs arranged side by side. Apparently this motif was first used in the north for it is in the carpets from Daghestan and Lesghistan that this pattern is found in its most pronounced form. Later the craftsmen of Kuba and Shirvan also adopted it.

It is worth remembering that northern Caucasian carpets have a coarser, and to some extent denser, layered backing, whereas carpets from Kuba and Shirvan usually have a finer backing in which the rows of weft threads can easily be distinguished.

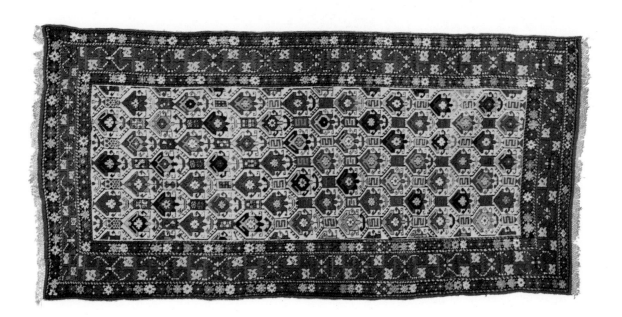

Caucasus. Daghestan region
End of 18th century. Knotted wool
50 × 103 in (127 × 262 cm)

Caucasus

Only a few of these carpets are in collections. A rug, very much like the one opposite, is in the Ballard Collection, Metropolitan Museum, New York.

In the arrangement of the central panel, with its cool colours rich in contrast, this carpet undoubtedly resembles the abstract pictures of our time. The design could be by Picasso, Miro or Klee. Yet all of them reflect some quality that collectors would regard as typically Caucasian. For a short time towards the end of the 18th century, there was a period when craftsmen overcame their usual *horror vacui* and designed carpets which were unique for the economy of their pentahedral ornamentation. Only a few carpets have survived from this period.

Caucasus. Kazak region
18th century. Knotted wool. Private collection, Milan
65 × 86½ in (165 × 220 cm)

Caucasus

Like the carpet on page 135 this one, too, comes from the northern Caucasus. Lesghis have a strongly ribbed backing in which the warp threads lie on two levels. They are made from a coarse wool, which allows the colours to appear especially rich in contrast. With their comparatively economic designs and accurate craftsmanship, Lesghi carpets are in great demand.

Caucasus. Lesghi region
19th century. Knotted wool
$39\frac{1}{4} \times 63$ in (100 × 160 cm)

Caucasus

Star motifs dominating the central panel are a typical feature of Lesghi carpets. This design appears to have been especially popular for it was adopted in other regions of the Caucasus too. Thus Lesghi stars in modified or similar form can also be found in carpets from Kuba and Shirvan. There are even Gandja and Kazak rugs with this motif.

Caucasus. Lesghi region
19th century. Knotted wool
$47\frac{1}{4} \times 100\frac{3}{4}$ in (120 × 256 cm)

Caucasus

The singular motif decorating the central panel opposite in a continuous pattern comes from the Karabagh region. Whether it is meant to represent stylized floral or animal shapes is hard to say. There is a definite flavour of scorpions or crustacea about it. The Islamic date 1115 has been knotted into the carpet.

In no other part of the Orient does a knotted date supply so much missing information about the age of the carpet. A comparison with other carpets of similar appearance will soon determine whether they were made at the same time as the dated rug.

Caucasus. Karabagh region. Goradis
18th century. Knotted wool. Private collection, Hamburg
$80\frac{3}{4} \times 131\frac{3}{4}$ in (205 × 335 cm). (Fragment)

151

Caucasus

Baku rugs occupy a special place in the hierarchy of Caucasian carpet groups. The range of colours is restricted to blues and yellows dominated by a strongly individual turquoise. Reds are avoided. The ornamentation also reveals idiosyncracies. The Turkoman regions across the Caspian Sea may well have exercised an influence. The carpet opposite displays an arrangement of octagons reminiscent of the early *güls* on Turkoman rugs. The octagon has also been quartered and each quarter filled with a bird-like motif. Carpets from this region are extremely rare. The delicate nuances of their colours, especially the vivid turquoise, gives them their considerable charm. Many attempts have been made to achieve this colour with chemical dyes. It is important to make sure that the colour runs evenly through the whole knot. On chemically treated carpets it is often weaker on the outside. If the colouring on the front of the rug is not the same as the colouring on the back, this also means that chemical dyes have been used.

Caucasus. Baku region. Surahani
Early 19th century. Knotted wool
$51\frac{1}{4} \times 72\frac{3}{4}$ in (130 × 185 cm)

153

Caucasus

Like the preceding carpet, this one is also striking for the design of the central panel which appears to consist of an alternating arrangement of prayer arches and polygons. Here, too, the ornamentation seems to reveal Turkoman influences from across the Caspian Sea. The cross motif in the polygons can often be seen in Turkoman rugs and the prayer arch in this rug is also rather like the arch in the prayer-rugs knotted by the Turkoman tribes of Beluchistan.

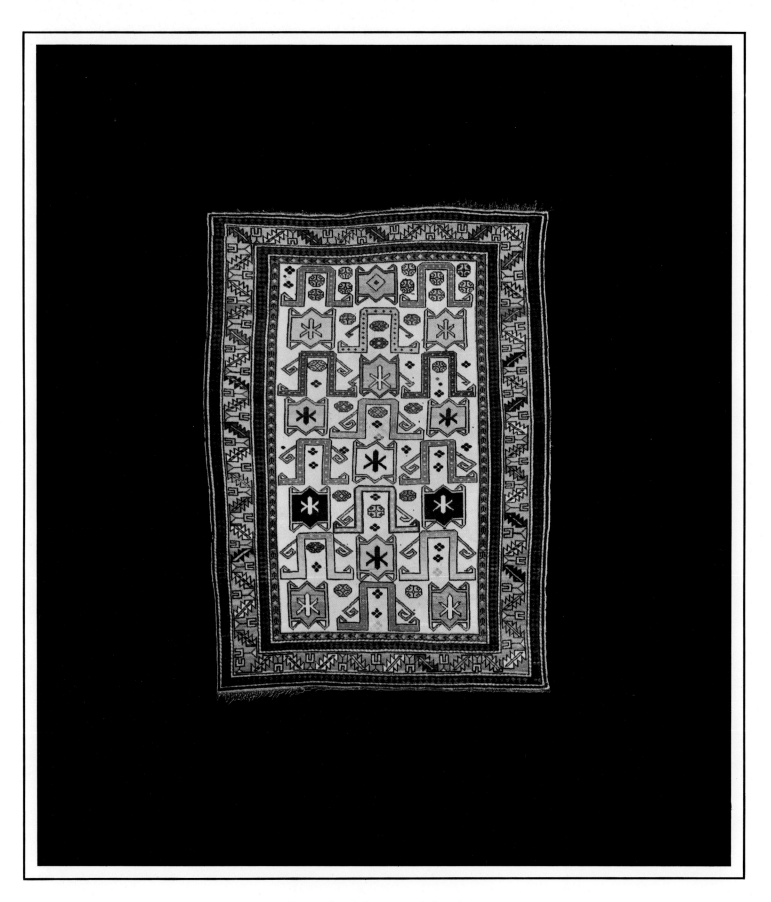

Caucasus. Baku region. Surahani
Early 19th century. Knotted wool
$45\frac{3}{4} \times 61\frac{1}{2}$ in (116×156 cm)

155

Caucasus

A completely plain, one-coloured central panel is often a feature of Talish carpets. However since Orientals, with their love of decoration, regard plain surfaces as an extravagance, they generally cannot resist scattering tiny decorations such as stars or, as here, animals, about the plain-coloured panel. Perhaps it is this which gives these carpets their particular charm.

This kind of carpet is known as Met-hane. More often than not the colour of the central panel is one of the many shades of blue, more rarely red and, very rarely indeed, green. Met-hane Talish carpets are particularly popular with collectors as they suit both old-fashioned and modern interiors.

Caucasus. Talish
About 1800. Knotted wool
41 × 95¼ in (104 × 242 cm)

157

Caucasus

One of the chief characteristics of these rugs which are popular both for their colours and design, is a rhomboid-shaped leaf pattern, filled with a rosette, with projecting tendrils. Realistically drawn floral motifs are only added in early pieces, like the one opposite. The age of the rug can also be deduced from the beetle-like ornament between the tendrils. The central panel is surrounded by the classical border with its pattern of reciprocal crenellations. The whole design is accurate and well balanced.

Caucasus. Karagashli
Early 19th century. Knotted wool. Private collection, Paris
41 × 100¾ in (104 × 256 cm)

Caucasus

The beetle-like motif in the rug on the preceding picture has now become a floral ornament surrounded by rays and set between medallions flanked by long tendrils. The vivid blue background is typical of Karagashli carpets. The white ground seen in the preceding rug is rare. The Kufic border is often seen in Anatolian as well as Caucasian carpets.

Caucasus. Karagashli
Mid 19th century. Knotted wool. Private collection, Hamburg
$47\frac{1}{4} \times 118$ in (120 × 300 cm)

Caucasus

Of the three Karagashlis shown, this one is the most characteristic. Sometimes there are only three leaf shapes surrounded by tendrils, the gaps filled with stars. There may also be two rows of such shapes placed side by side. Almost always the shining blue background is surrounded by a main border of a contrasting yellow in which the leaf and chalice motif is repeated. All Karagashlis are finely woven, with a low pile and shimmering colours.

Caucasus. Karagashli
Mid 19th century. Knotted wool
$40\frac{1}{2} \times 63\frac{1}{4}$ in (103×161 cm)

Caucasus

Mythological animals in more or less geometrical form appear in many Caucasian carpets. In none do they stand out so clearly as in this Akstafa rug. The central panel consists of six rows of such winged mythological creatures separated by decorative bands. The so-called Kufic border, accompanied by a narrow outer S-border, surrounds the central panel. The colours betray a Baku influence.

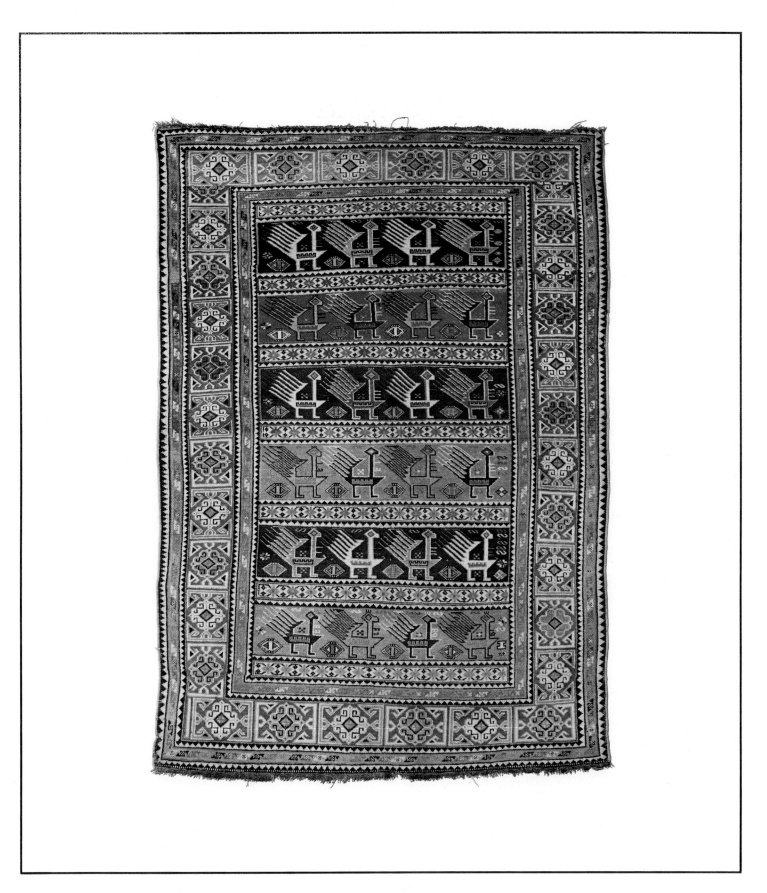

Caucasus. Akstafa
Mid 19th century. Knotted wool
$51\frac{1}{4} \times 71\frac{1}{4}$ in (130 × 181 cm)

Caucasus

When the talk is of Kuba rugs, the supposition is always of rugs with a background colour ranging from dark blue to a glowing mid-blue. A red background is very much rarer. A green or a yellow one is very rare indeed. This magnificent Kuba displays a continuous pattern of floral motifs combined with stars on the yellow background of its central panel.

Caucasus. Kuba
First half of 19th century. Knotted wool. Private collection, Paris
$34\frac{1}{2} \times 81$ in (88×206 cm)

Caucasus

The Genjeh region must surely have produced the widest variety of rugs for both quality and style in the Caucasus. At one end of the scale are the coarse, crudely knotted rustic rugs, at the other the finest, most painstakingly worked carpets. Its central situation, surrounded by Kazak, Karabagh and Shirvan, may be the main reason for the versatility of its designs. The age of the rug opposite is revealed by the border with its bewitching, constantly changing pastel shades. The diagonal rows of stars in the central panel shows its kinship with the neighbouring Talish rugs. The fine, silky wool makes the delicate colours harmonize most effectively.

Caucasus. Genjeh region
18th century. Knotted wool
44 × 109 in (112 × 277 cm)

Caucasus

With its narrow border and pentahedral arrangement of octagons, this unusual carpet could still be a product of the 18th century. Originally it was a bit longer. The pieces have been joined by a master craftsman in such a way that the breaks are invisible. The texture of the knotting is extraordinarily fine for Kazak or Genjeh work and is an indication that this is an early piece of the Caucasian craft.

Caucasus. Kazak or Genjeh region
Mid 19th century. Knotted wool
$40\frac{1}{2} \times 60\frac{1}{4}$ in (103 $\times$ 153 cm)

Caucasus

The ornamentation and colours in this rug, especially those of the border, are unusual. It would probably still be right to give it an 18th-century date. The rows of borders filled with boteh motifs decorating the central panel are often encountered in Kazak rugs—but never displaying such a unique combination of colours.

Caucasus. Kazak region
18th to 19th century. Knotted wool. Private collection, Hamburg
55 × 89¾ in (140 × 228 cm)

167

Caucasus

In the Caucasus changes of style have also been reflected in the design of carpets. Towards the end of the 18th century there was a short period when carpets with simple divisions and economical patterns predominated. To this group belongs the rug opposite which displays on a red ground a rhomboid in different colours but almost exactly similar shapes. Pieces like this are in great demand by collectors as they are unquestionably very old.

Caucasus. Kazak
About 1800. Knotted wool
$65 \times 111\frac{1}{2}$ in (165×283 cm)

169

Caucasus

This Kazak rug belongs to the same group of carpets with simple designs and little ornamentation. Like many of the earlier examples, it has a border which is extremely narrow in comparison with the central panel. The central panel itself makes a powerful effect because of the sharp contrast in the positioning of the blue, white and red colours. This conveys all the primitive strength of Caucasian carpet design.

Caucasus. Kazak
About 1800. Knotted wool
57 × 67 in (145 × 170 cm)

Caucasus

One of the most interesting things about this carpet is the central panel. It looks as if there are four cows facing each other in the design. This, plus the use of cochineal in some of the polygons, means that this must be a very early piece of work. A similar carpet was exhibited in November 1971 at the Kazak Exhibition, New York, by Raoul Tschebull (Plate 40 in the catalogue).

Caucasus. Kazak region
About 1800. Knotted wool
74 × 49½ in (188 × 226 cm)

171

Caucasus

In contrast to the preceding pieces, the central panel of this carpet is covered with a wealth of decorations which almost conceals the fact that it is a carpet with a prayer niche. The construction of the design was clearly subject to a strong artistic discipline and conveys the impression of a flower-covered meadow divided into squares.

The decorations, especially the cartouches, point to an origin in Bordjalou. Note the abstract linear drawing in the long sides of the main border, whilst the short sides display a more naturalistic leaf tendril.

Caucasus. Bordjalou
First half of 19th century. Knotted wool
$46\frac{1}{2}$ × 56 in (118 × 142 cm)

Caucasus

There are comparatively few small Kazaks which can compare
with the rug below. At the Kazak exhibition in New York, organ-
ized by Raoul Tschebull in 1971, there was a number of small
Kazak rugs which were very similar to the one below both in
colour and construction. The simple design and impressive colours
of the border make a harmonious frame round the central panel
with its sparse—and thus all the more effective—ornamentation.

Caucasus. Bordjalou. Kazak
Mid 19th century. Knotted wool
$48\frac{1}{2} \times 59$ in (123 × 150 cm)

174

Caucasus

In both this picture and the next, the yellowish, almost lime-green colour gives the carpets their distinction. The small dots in the red central panel and the almost black corners filled with hooked shapes are also worthy of attention.

Caucasus. Kazak region
First half of 19th century. Knotted wool. Private collection, Hamburg
67 × 90¼ in (170 × 230 cm)

Caucasus

There are many Kazak rugs with a design like this, in which the central motif is surrounded by four squares. What is remarkable about the carpet opposite is the green background and its archaic border. Both point to a very early date for the carpet.

Collectors can often judge the age of a green carpet from its tone—the more yellow it is the older the carpet is likely to be. Some strips of *Abrash* (streaks in the main colour) may even be a light lime-green. In later pieces the green is darker and more uniform, ending with the deep bottle-green of 20th century carpets.

Caucasus. Kazak region. Karajov
Mid 19th century. Knotted wool. Private collection, Hamburg
$72\frac{3}{4} \times 86\frac{3}{4}$ in (185 × 225 cm)

177

Caucasus

In this enchanting little rug, it is easy to recognize motifs from 17th century Caucasian dragon carpets. The Kufic border is also an indication of its age. The texture of the knotting is very fine and, considering its small format, the rug manages to achieve a remarkable harmony of colour and pattern.

Caucasus. Shirvan region
Early 19th century. Knotted wool. Private collection, Bergisch-Gladbach
$38\frac{1}{2} \times 52\frac{3}{4}$ in (98 × 134 cm)

Caucasus

It is hard to decide what is most attractive about this rug: the extremely simple design of the central panel with its clear colours or the enchanting stepped border which displays a vivid range of tones rarely found in Caucasian carpets.

Caucasus. Shirvan region
First half of 19th century. Knotted wool. Private collection, Paris
$35 \times 52\frac{1}{4}$ in (89×133 cm)

Caucasus

It is rare to find Caucasian carpets with a central panel containing such a fine filigree design below and a clearly defined prayer arch. The manifold, very realistically drawn, household utensils almost look as if they belonged in a child's toy box. They are proof of the extraordinarily fine knotting without which such a playful effect could not have been achieved. In contrast to the central panel the form and coloration of the border are typical of those in Caucasian carpets generally.

Caucasus. Shirvan
About 1800. Knotted wool
35 × 56 in (89 × 142 cm)

Caucasus

This rug will always stand out from the many which were made in the Shirvan region during the 18th and 19th centuries. The enchanting pastel colours on a white background in the border contrast with the lively red of the central panel and the deep blue of the innermost field. The floral motifs in the border and the central panel are unusually simplified and rounded off. The flowering bush in the centre does not really belong to the normal repertoire of Shirvan carpet designs. The sharpness of outline can only be achieved by a low pile and very fine knotting.

Caucasus. Marasali. Shirvan
About 1800. Knotted wool
$47\frac{1}{4} \times 55$ in (120 × 140 cm)

Caucasus

This carpet, too, is a tribute to the accuracy and imagination of its maker. The main border reproduces a realistic design of blossoms, whilst the central panel restricts itself to a continuous pattern of angular shapes. As so often, it is the colour combination of contrasts that gives this carpet its charm.

Caucasus. Kuba region
Mid 19th century. Knotted wool
$39\frac{1}{4} \times 47\frac{1}{4}$ in (100 × 120 cm)

Caucasus

A close look at the design of the central panel reveals that, as in the carpet on the previous page, it is composed of an arrangement of hexagons, though here they are not extended but look as if they have been cut out of a circle. Blue and red are the colours most commonly used for the background of the central panel in the Kuba region. The clear yellow of this rug is most unusual. The floral and beam motifs of the main border seem to indicate a Tshitshi origin. The carpet is extremely finely knotted, with an unusually high pile, and is finished off at each end with the Soumak stitch commonly used in the Kuba region.

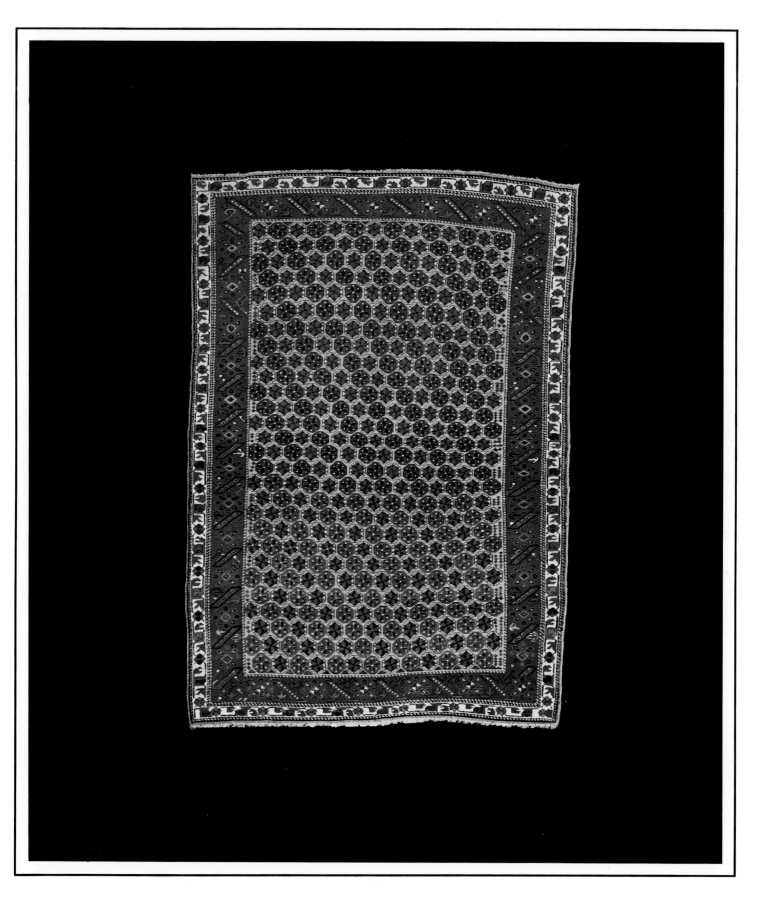

Caucasus. Kuba region
Early 19th century. Knotted wool
$47\frac{1}{4} \times 66$ in (120 × 168 cm)

Caucasus

The central panel of the carpet unmistakably still displays the dragon-phoenix motif in abstract form with the great white, green and turquoise lancet-shaped leaves of the 17th-century dragon carpets.

Soumak rugs justly continue to become ever more popular. They are not just made in the Daghestan regions but also in Kuba, Shirvan and Genjeh. The age of these woven carpets can be traced by their colour range. The older the carpet, the lighter, brighter and more contrasting are the colours. The overall impression is darker in later pieces until in the most recent examples they have degenerated into a depressing dark brown-red-blue object.

Caucasus. Daghestan region. Soumak
18th century. Woven wool. Private collection, Bergisch-Gladbach
96 × 132½ in (244 × 335 cm)

Caucasus

The S-design, which extends all over the carpet in different colours, is an abstraction of the dragon motif. The feet of the dragon are still visible in the lower part of the S, whilst a fine line in the upper part just gives a hint of the dragon's horns. In carpets older than this one it is easier to recognize the dragon and the colours are lighter and more cheerful. A characteristic of Sille carpets is that they generally consist of two parts sewn together lengthways. Perhaps they were used as door hangings.

Caucasus. Daghestan region. Sille
19th century. Woven wool
$88\frac{1}{2} \times 181\frac{1}{2}$ in (225×462 cm). (Partial view)

189

Caucasus

It is not easy to guess the original purpose of this narrow piece of embroidery worked in silk on linen. Most probably the medallion lay on a table or a plinth, or perhaps a prayer desk, whilst the two ends, each embroidered with a prayer arch design, hung down on either side. The yellow panel stands out from the red filigree work and is unlike most other Caucasian work both for its delicacy of line and the unusual nature of its motifs. Another unusual feature is that the two rectangles embroidered on the same background are differently drawn.

A number of beautiful embroideries from the 17th and 18th centuries have survived, several examples of which can be seen in the book *Caucasian Rugs*.

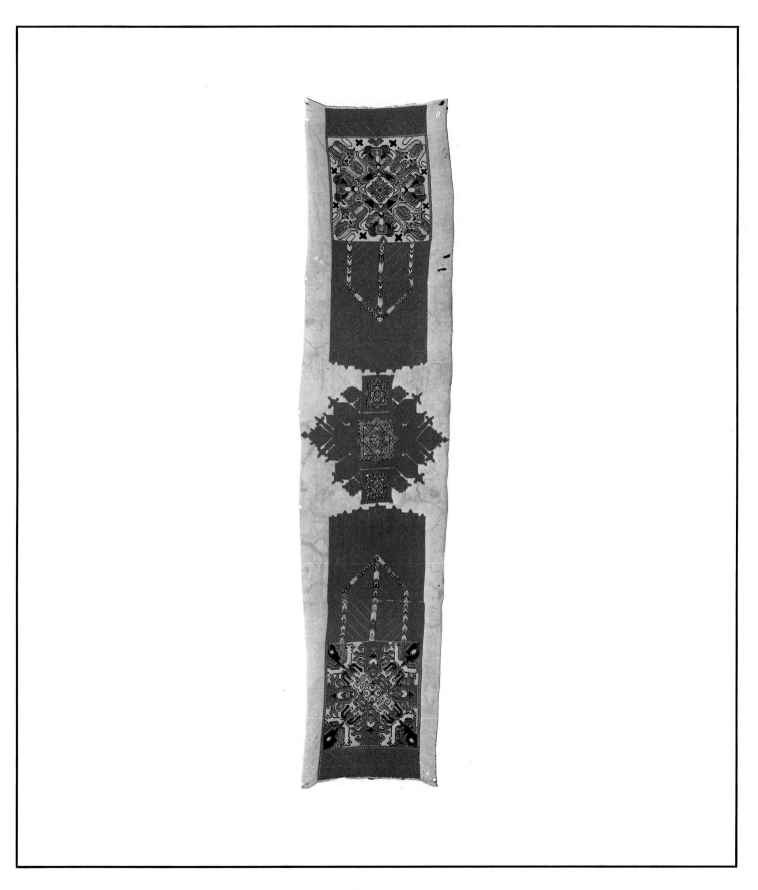

Caucasus
17th century. Silk embroidery
15 × 72¾ in (38 × 185 cm)

Armenia

In private collections and books on rugs, it is sometimes possible to find pictures of carpets which contain a mixture of Anatolian and Caucasian motifs. Originally they may have been late descendants of the 16th century Persian hunting rugs. Although they are charming, they lack the balance and purity of style of the originals.

Armenian. Animal rug
18th century. Knotted wool. Private collection, Milan
64 × 136¾ in (163 × 347 cm)

Armenia

As in the preceding carpet, motifs from the most different places come together in this piece. The border is Anatolian and can be compared with rugs made in the Ladik region, whilst the central panel shows a mixture of motifs from Caucasia and northern Persia. Its colours are exquisite and provide interesting evidence of its age.

Armenian carpet
18th century. Knotted wool. Private collection, Hamburg
$60\frac{1}{2} \times 114$ in (154 × 290 cm)

Turkestan

For years Beluchi carpets were less highly regarded than they deserved to be. Until just before the Second World War it was possible to buy quantities of interesting antique Beluchis comparatively cheaply. Nowadays it is hard to find one good rug. Beluchis only appear monotonous in colour and uniform in design. A closer look reveals that even within the limited range of their colours there is an immense number of variations, a tribute to the inventive imagination of the craftsman who made them. It is characteristic of old Beluchis that the *kilim* strips at each end of the rug are worked with great care. They are often woven in different colours and designs.

Turkoman carpet. Beluchi
Early 19th century. Knotted wool
$39\frac{1}{4} \times 61$ in (100×155 cm)

Turkestan

The tree-of-life motif on a camelhair ground at once strikes the eye. It is also a good example of a rug with meticulously worked *kilims* at each end.

Turkoman carpet. Beluchi
19th century. Knotted wool
$34\frac{1}{2} \times 49\frac{1}{2}$ in (88 × 125 cm)

Turkestan

Turkoman carpets, known to dealers as 'Bokhara rugs', are, in fact, knotted by many different tribes. The *gül* device, as chief ornament of the central panel, is, however, typical of them all. Thus there are 'Tekke' *güls*, 'Saryk' *güls*, 'Yomud' *güls*, 'Salor' *güls* and 'Chaudor' *güls*. In the carpet opposite, the chief *gül* of the Chaudors has become a subsidiary *gül*, whilst allowing the chief *gül* of the Chubbashi (apparently a subsidiary tribe of the Chaudors) to predominate. These carpets are more loosely knotted and feel softer than those of the Tekke or other Turkoman tribes.

Turkestan. Chaudor-Turkoman
19th century. Knotted wool. McCoy Jones Collection, Washington
$84\frac{1}{2} \times 100\frac{3}{4}$ in (214 × 256 cm)

Turkestan

Chaudor carpets stand out from the normal run of Turkoman rugs by their unusual brown-black background colour. The central panel is usually covered by a rhomboid-shaped network in which the colour of the diagonal lines changes. The carpets are usually about 72 in (183 cm) broad and 108 in (275 cm) in length but can be much longer than this.

This is the first time it has been possible to reproduce such an unusually small rug in this genre. Here the colours are not arranged for contrast diagonally, but in a star shape. The border is also much more geometric than usual. The colours however are traditional. Note the care with which the *kilim* has been embroidered at each end.

Turkestan. Chaudor, Turkoman
19th century. Knotted wool
$43\frac{3}{4} \times 91\frac{3}{4}$ in (111 × 205 cm)

Turkestan

The Kyzyl-Ayak are members of a Turkoman tribe producing very
individual carpets as to colour and design. They generally made
use of a dark-toned *Hatchli* design (cross shape, dividing the main
panel into four quarters), finished off with a brownish strip at the
bottom. However, the Kyzyl-Ayak also made larger carpets, including prayer rugs like the one opposite. It is always their unusual
design, or the particular grouping of colours that distinguish the
Kyzyl-Ayak work from all other Turkoman carpets. A point to
watch is that the white sections are frequently knotted in cotton
and the magenta-coloured sections in silk.

Turkestan. Kyzyl-Ayak-Turkoman
19th century. Knotted wool
$38\frac{1}{2} \times 57$ in (97 × 145 cm)

Turkestan

This carpet must have caused a sensation even in its own country. The fine texture of the knotting and the silky wool are unsurpassed. On top of that there are the unusual and magnificent colours in a range not usually used in Turkestan. The accurate, realistic working of the leaf and flower motifs in the lower part of the rug shows that this is a very old piece. The dark blue, almost black background colour of the end strip sets this rug apart from all others of its kind. *Hatchli* means 'cross' and refers to the quartered central panel.

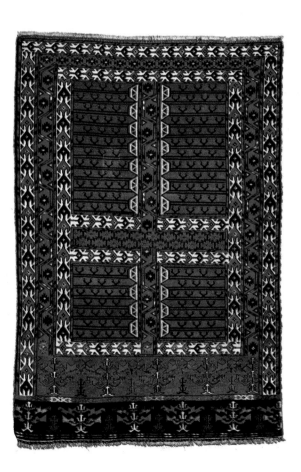

Turkestan. Yomud-Hatchli
Early 19th century. Knotted wool. Private collection, Paris
48½ × 71 in (123 × 180 cm)

Turkestan

In this carpet, too, the end strip changes its colour from red to blue if not in quite such a striking way as in the preceding one. Here there are no floral motifs but a design generally described as 'Yomud fir'. The central panel, quartered by a cross, displays rhomboid-shaped rosettes instead of the more usual chalice shapes.

Turkestan. Yomud-Hatchli
19th century. Knotted wool
$46\frac{1}{2} \times 62$ in (118 × 157 cm)

Turkestan

The design and colouring of Tekke-Hatchli are usually more monotonous than those of the Kyzyl-Ayak or Yomud. It is rare for the end strip to be designed with so much imagination as this one. Small trees outlined in red, blue and white, compose the lower part of the carpet before the actual end strip begins. In contrast to the two preceding pieces, there is an arch in the top part which either represents a yurt or a prayer arch. It is not yet known what function these hatchli rugs had. The majority of authorities assume that they were tent carpets. Others maintain that the arch points to its use as a prayer rug. Perhaps they were used for both, as some hatchli rugs are so small that they would scarcely be suitable for door curtains.

Turkestan. Tekke-Hatchli
19th century. Knotted wool
51 × 60¼ in (130 × 153 cm)

Turkestan

In the book *Central Asian Rugs* by this author, two beautiful examples of Turkoman craft are reproduced. A somewhat smaller rug, in superlative condition, with unusually brilliant colours, is shown here. It is wrong to think that the colours in Turkoman rugs need necessarily be monotonous, even dull. The older a Turkoman rug is, the more colourful it is likely to be; the red is apt to be lighter and more fiery in every tone. When, as in this carpet, there are also some areas worked in magenta-coloured silk, the artistic effect reaches its peak.

The row of figures in the niches are not easy to identify. It is not clear whether they are floral motifs or the childish drawings of a little man, for there does appear to be a head complete with mouth, nose and eyes, arms with clearly defined hands, legs with feet. Research into Turkoman carpets seems to reveal that probably during the early days of the craft, animals, especially birds, formed part of the pattern rather than plant forms.

Turkestan. Salor. Tent bag
About 1800. Knotted wool
$19\frac{3}{4} \times 48\frac{3}{4}$ in (50 × 124 cm)

207

Turkestan

There have always been a great many tent and camel bags. They were used in the tents of the nomadic and semi-nomadic tribes for storing things as well as for decoration. The women who knotted them vied with each other to produce the most beautiful bags. It is therefore hardly surprising that they are generally the most finely knotted objects produced in that country. The bag pictured opposite is a particularly handsome piece, whose great age is indicated by the realistically worked little trees at the lower end.

Turkestan. Tekke tent bag
First half of 19th century. Knotted wool
$26\frac{3}{4} \times 48\frac{3}{4}$ in (68 × 124 cm)

Turkestan

This bag can be dated most easily by the greater range of its colours and its brighter, more contrasting tones. In addition, there is the fine texture of the knotting and the accuracy of the design. Here the side *güls* are almost more interesting than the chief *gül*. The strip at the bottom also denotes imagination and individuality.

Turkestan. Yomud-Turkoman
19th century. Knotted wool
$30\frac{3}{4} \times 45\frac{1}{4}$ in (78 × 115 cm)

Turkestan

This little bag is unmistakable proof of the enchanting effect which can be produced with a minimum of design. The big, plain-coloured areas are interrupted by sharply drawn *güls*, the side *güls* merely being indicated by lines. A charming border surrounds the work like a frame.

Turkestan. Yomud-Turkoman
19th century. Knotted wool. Private collection, Gallenmüller, Bonn

Turkestan

Pentagonal camel bags are called *osmolduk*. Generally they are decorated with a simple barred pattern. The Yomud fir on this bag has been drawn in an uncommonly wide variety of colours. As a rule, the older a Turkoman bag is, the brighter are the colours. In addition to the otherwise atonal red and blue, the following tones have been added in silk: light red, orange, yellow, light blue, green-blue and, sometimes, pink.

Turkestan. Yomud-Osmolduk
Mid 19th century. Knotted wool. Private collection, Paris
30 × 50¾ in (76 × 129 cm)

Turkestan

The rugs made by the Karakalpak, a nomadic Turkoman tribe in North Turkestan, are characteristic of all nomadic rugs: they are unevenly worked, coarsely knotted and have vivid colours which do not always go well together. The comparative scarcity of these rugs in Europe should stimulate collectors to take advantage of any chance that offers itself to acquire one.

Turkestan. Karakalpak
19th century. Knotted wool. Private collection, St Gallen
$72\frac{3}{4} \times 129$ in (185×328 cm)

Turkestan

Karakalpak rugs have preserved an original tradition of design
in spite of proximity to other Turkoman tribes. Although they are
knotted more coarsely, and their colours are richer in contrast,
they reveal an imaginative strength and colouring often found in
nomadic rugs. Notice the strong use of yellow in the collectors'
piece opposite and the great care with which the astonishingly
colourful *kilim* has been carried out.

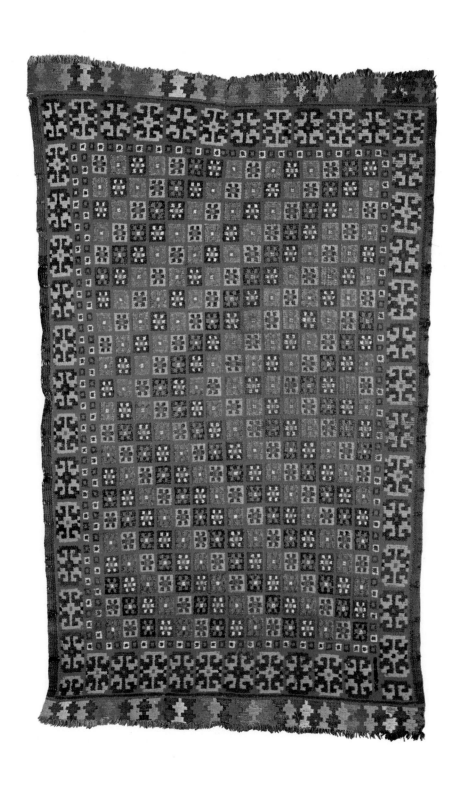

Turkestan. Karakalpak
19th century. Knotted wool
$37 \times 58\frac{1}{4}$ in (94 × 148 cm)

Turkestan

The knotted rugs of the Beshir are easy to distinguish from those of the other Turkoman tribes. They use a far wider range of colours, including a greater predominance of yellow, and avoid purely geometric decorations. Floral motifs, leaves and tendrils are introduced into their designs. It is hardly surprising that Beshir rugs find special favour with collectors.

Turkestan. Beshir tent bag
19th century. Knotted wool. Private collection, Cologne
$37\frac{1}{2} \times 63\frac{3}{4}$ in (95 × 162 cm)

Turkestan

As so often in Beshir rugs, a strictly geometrical pattern is combined with floral motifs. In the piece shown below, the central panel has been divided into differently coloured squares, each square being filled with a floral motif. The main border, with its elegant pattern of blossoms, is in direct contrast and perhaps, for this reason, gives the rug its charm. It is one of the oldest rugs to survive from this district.

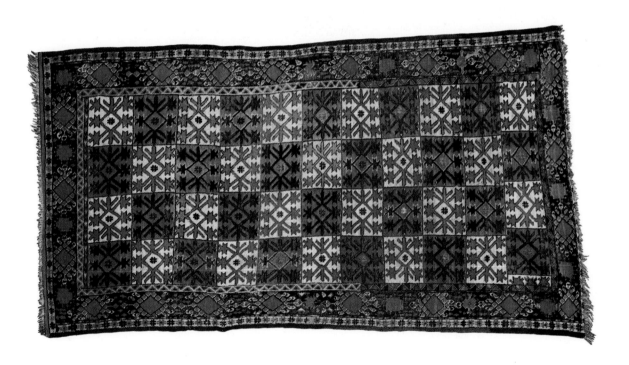

Turkestan. Beshir
About 1800. Knotted wool. Private collection, Cologne
$46\frac{3}{4} \times 78\frac{1}{4}$ in (119 × 199 cm)

Turkestan

Like the preceding rug, this piece displays a simple, basic pattern of small squares filled with tiny, brightly coloured flowers. What is unusual about it is that it does not really have a border, the pattern of squares going right to the edge. This rug may have been knotted as early as the 18th century.

Turkestan. Beshir
Early 19th century. Knotted wool. Private collection, Cologne
59 × 87 in (150 × 221 cm)

219

Turkestan

This prayer rug with its unusual design displays a row of decorative symbols which seems to originate from a number of different tribal traditions. The basic structure is most like that of the Tekke rugs, although similar ones have also been made in Northern Afghanistan. On the other hand, the use of yellow, and the regular design of the central panel, is reminiscent of the carpets made by the Ersari of Beshir. Then there are the small patches of cochineal at the lower end of the rug, a colour which is common—although only used for small areas—in Salor rugs. All in all, this is an interesting and unusual carpet which should interest collectors because of its extreme rarity.

Turkestan. Ersari
19th century. Knotted wool
56 × 68 in (142 × 173 cm)

Turkestan

It is common knowledge, nowadays, that no rugs were knotted in Bokhara itself, but that the name of this town was adopted as a collective description for Turkoman rugs because of its position as the centre of distribution. In Bokhara itself, however, and between this town and Samarkand, there lived Uzbek tribes who have made a name for themselves with their wonderful silk embroideries on a finely woven linen background. The design of the knotted rug below has certainly been influenced by Bokhara embroidery. No other example of this type of knotted carpet is known.

Turkestan. Uzbek knotted carpet
About 1800. Knotted wool
63 × 58¾ in (160 × 149 cm)

Afghanistan

In his book on oriental carpets, Grote-Hasenborg has already commented on the beauty and rarity of the carpets knotted by the Saryks of Afghanistan. Only a very few pieces have survived. The almost circular *gül* (rose) device, combined with the angular shapes in the border, are characteristic features. What is really conclusive, however, is the fine, silky wool which unfortunately no reproduction can adequately convey.

Afghanistan. Saryk-Turkoman
Early 19th century. Knotted wool. Private collection, Cologne
$91\frac{3}{4} \times 114\frac{1}{4}$ in (205 × 290 cm)

Afghanistan

This Afghan rug has the same gleaming, silky wool as the one on the preceding page. The almost blue-black ground is in contrast to the characteristic *gül* ornament. The narrow border displays floral motifs in alternating colours, a combination which is rarely found in Turkoman carpets. In its design and colouring this piece must be unique.

Afghanistan. Guchan
19th century. Knotted wool
45¼ × 84¾ in (115 × 215 cm)

East Turkestan

During the days of the Moghul Empire beautiful carpets with a dense floral design were knotted in east Turkestan and India. The piece shown below bears witness to the skill and elegance which reigned in Samarkand in those days. The original rug must have been approximately double the size. Only a few examples of this courtly craft have survived.

East Turkestan. Kashgar
17th century. Knotted silk. Private collection, Cologne
$89\frac{3}{4} \times 98\frac{1}{2}$ in (228×250 cm). (Fragment)

East Turkestan

During the 17th century carpets were made in the Kashgar and Yarkand regions which, for luxury, extravagance and artistic accomplishment are fully the equal of all that is best in Persian craftsmanship. The rug opposite comes from the collection of P. J. Morgan, New York, and is the only known complete example of this genre. Fragments of a similar carpet which, however, was made much later in Khotan, are in the Museum of Crafts in Frankfurt-am-Main. A detailed description of this carpet was recently published in the *Festschrift* for Professor Dr P. W. Meister.

East Turkestan. Yarkand
17th century. Knotted silk with metal threads
$87\frac{1}{2} \times 155$ in (222×394 cm)

East Turkestan

The so-called Samarkand area covers the products of three places: Kashgar, Yarkand and Khotan. The Khotan carpet opposite, is one of the oldest known pieces. A pomegranate, which could not be bettered for elegance and accuracy of design, is shown growing out of a blue vase on the lower part of the rug. This one-sided, ascending pattern dates the rug for in later pieces the same design grows out of two vases, one at each end of the rug, to meet in the centre.

Few oriental rugs have suffered more from the use of aniline and other industrial dyes. After a while the colours in Khotan rugs clashed so luridly that most of them were given a chemical wash. In some cases this not only bleached out all the colours, but also affected the already rather loose knotting, making them even less durable. It is therefore hardly surprising that most of these chemically treated rugs have been worn down to the basic weave although they are scarcely more than 50 years old.

East Turkestan. Khotan
18th century. Knotted wool. Private collection, Cologne
$45\frac{3}{4} \times 50\frac{1}{4}$ in (116 × 128 cm)

India

Well known everywhere, and in great demand, are the so-called embroideries from Bokhara which, from the 17th century until recent times, were made by the Uzbeks of central Asia in the region between Bokhara and Samarkand. They are unique for the subtlety of their colour and design.

When the Moghuls conquered India, they imported skilled craftsmen from Persia and central Asia into India in order to build up a carpet industry there. Certainly there must have been Uzbek craftsmen among them who created embroideries in India which, in technique and colouring, though they may be seen to have an Uzbek origin, nevertheless betray an Indian influence. The rug opposite is a superb example of this. The decoration of the *mihrab* corresponds to the skilful workmanship in Indian carpets of the same period, i.e. under Moghul domination.

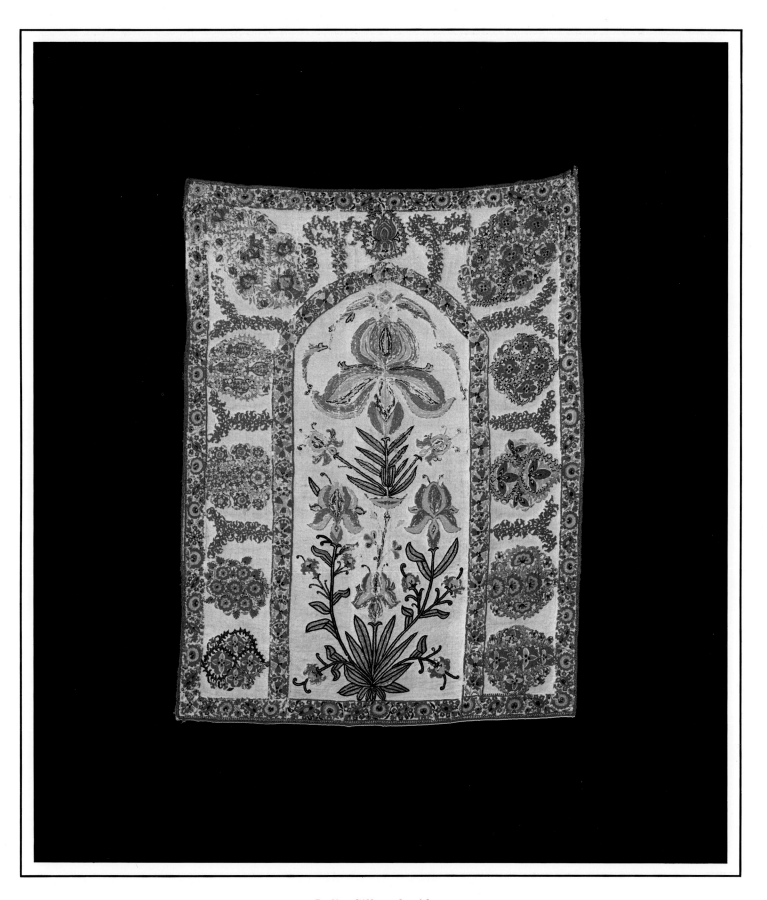

India. Silk embroidery
17th century. Silk worked on linen
$39\frac{1}{4} \times 52\frac{1}{4}$ in (100 × 133 cm)

India

Beautiful carpets were made in India, at first by the Persian crafts-men introduced by the Moghul emperors. Later, during the 17th century, there was a change of style when purely Indian motifs began to appear. At Masulipatam in the south, Indian, Persian and even, as shown opposite, Mameluke motifs might be used. A similar carpet is in the Ballard Collection, in the Metropolitan Museum, New York.

India. Masulipatam
17th century. Knotted wool
52 × 81 in (132 × 206 cm)

India

If the preceding carpet still shows a mixture of Persian and Middle Eastern influences, the more naturalistic Indian ornamentation has prevailed in the one opposite. Realistically drawn sprigs of flowers fill the network of the central panel.

The various Indian carpets are as different in structure from each other as are all the other oriental knotted carpets. Those made in Lahore are thin, medium-fine and rather granular to the touch. Agra carpets have a longer pile, on a very densely woven backing and feel stiffer. In Masulipatam the rugs are semi-fine, have a very short touch and, because of their comparatively thin warp, feel rather hard.

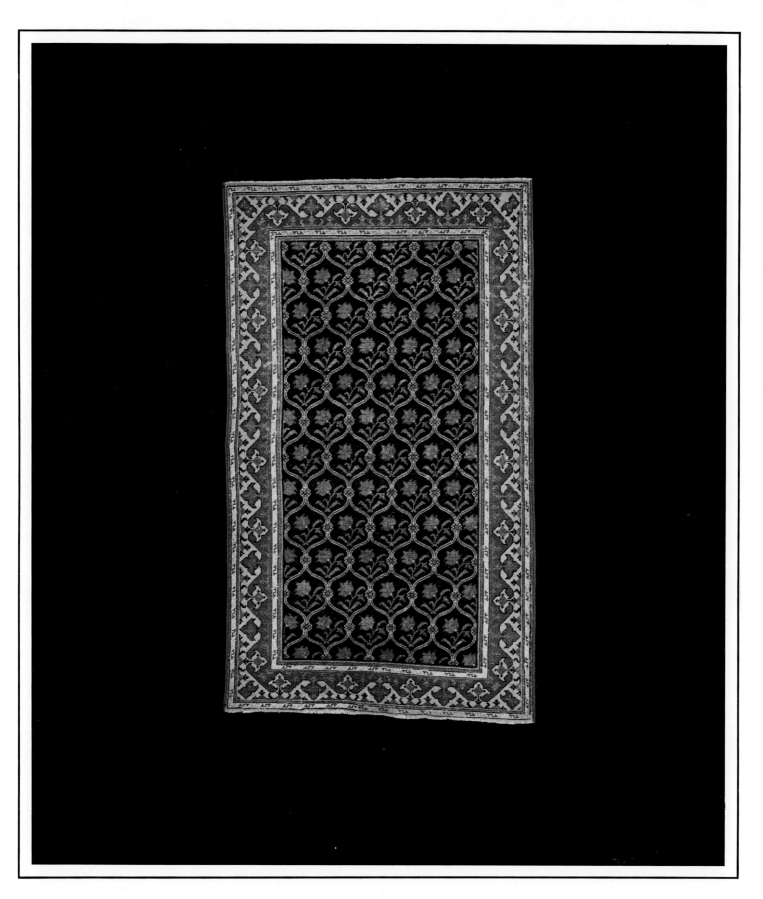

India. Masulipatam
17th to 18th century. Knotted wool
$39\frac{1}{4} \times 65\frac{1}{4}$ in (100 × 166 cm)

235

China

The design and colouring of Chinese carpets is so different from all other oriental rugs that even the layman can distinguish them at once. The range of colours is restricted, with light and dark blue, yellow and apricot predominating. The motifs are composed of realistic floral decorations in the central panel, framed by a geometric, linear design in the borders.

Little is known about the origin of Chinese carpets. It is doubtful whether knotted carpets were made there before the 17th century. Certainly felt carpets, decorated with appliqué work, were made before then and it seems likely that the habit of clipping the pile round the motifs on carpets manufactured in Pao-Tao and Peking dates back to this old type of appliqué work. As in all Chinese crafts symbolism plays an important role. Every colour, blossom, dragon or phoenix—in short every bit of ornamentation—has a symbolic meaning.

China. Ning Hsia
About 1700. Knotted wool
$101\frac{1}{4} \times 118$ in (257×300 cm)

China

Chinese works of art are dated by the name of the emperor who was reigning at the time of their manufacture. The 18th century carpet opposite contains a unique combination of a geometric medallion with archaic dragon heads in the centre which is echoed in the corners of the central panel. The very delicately graded colours are reminiscent of the porcelain made during the same epoch. A point to remember is that the grey dye used in the outer border of antique Chinese carpets is liable to decompose the wool.

China. Ning Hsia
Chien-Lung period. Knotted wool
54 × 76 in (137 × 193 cm)

239

China

Elegant blue and beige carpets were made in Pao-Tao. They can be distinguished from those of Ning Hsia by the comparatively close knotting on a smaller number of weft threads. Apart from this, Ning Hsia rugs have a fairly long, silky pile whereas the pile on Pao-Tao rugs is much shorter and the wool is denser and more durable.

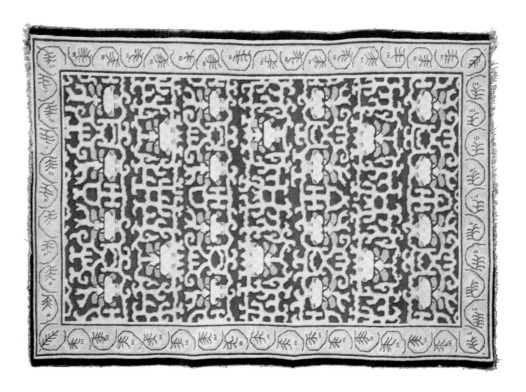

China. Pao-Tao
About 1800. Knotted wool. Private collection, Cologne
$72\frac{3}{4} \times 103\frac{1}{4}$ in (185 × 262 cm)

China

A feature of Chinese rugs, as also of the rarer ones from Mongolia, is that the weft threads were often run across the rug so that the fringed ends appeared on the long sides rather than the short ones. Yellow and apricot seem to have been favourite colours for the background. It is said that the use of a certain lustrous yellow was only permitted for work ordered by the emperor's household.

China. Ning Hsia
About 1800. Knotted wool
50 × 78 in (127 × 198 cm)

China

Symbolism plays an important role in Chinese carpets, as well as in Chinese life. The bats which are scattered over the central panel of this rug, and which alternate with bands of clouds, are supposed to bring luck. The apricot-coloured background of the central panel is in harmonious contrast to the yellow-green border with its meandering pattern. This carpet exudes an atmosphere of peace and harmony. Its state of preservation is excellent.

China. Ning Hsia
Early 19th century. Knotted wool
$65\frac{1}{4} \times 100\frac{1}{4}$ in (166×255 cm)

243

China

A great many of the carpets knotted in Ning Hsia appear to have been exported to neighbouring Tibet. On the stone benches in the monasteries, square sitting pads of exactly similar design lay linked together in chains which sometimes reached considerable lengths. Ten or twelve such pads linked together was not an uncommon sight. When these narrow carpets reached Europe the dealers may well have had doubts about their age as they always looked quite new underneath. In order to resolve such doubts, it is as well to remember that these rugs, like the pillar rugs of Tibet, were quilted with blue linen or silk and so do not show the usual signs of ageing such as fading, etc.

China. Ning Hsia
About 1800. Knotted wool
32 × 61¾ in (81 × 157 cm)

245

China

To the inhabitants of Mongolia and China, the horse represented one of their most valuable possessions. It is hardly surprising, therefore, that even the saddle covers which decorated the horse, should have been knotted in silk and wool. The famous McMullan Collection in New York contains a great many such saddle covers. Many of them still have the holes through which the saddle-horns were drawn. To prevent the legs of the rider from rubbing the pile, these rugs were knotted in two separate parts with the pile in each running downwards. Then the two parts would be sewn together down the centre. As all rugs display various degrees of brightness depending on whether one is looking into the pile or along it, such saddle rugs display both light effects at once.

China. Ning-Hsia saddle cover
19th century. Knotted silk. Private collection, Cologne
$29\frac{1}{4} \times 58\frac{3}{4}$ in (74 × 149 cm)